**QTS MATH**

 **QTS LITERA**

Practice for your

QTS Skills

Test

8 Full Practice Tests

David Chryssides

TABLE OF CONTENTS

How to use this book

This QTS skills test book provides practice questions within a test format for both the numeracy and literacy skills test. You can work through each test in exam conditions or just practise the questions in your own time. After completing a test, we think it is useful to check all your answers to see which questions you have answered incorrectly, to help you determine the areas you need to work on before moving on to the next test. The practice tests are intended to help you identify areas of weakness but also indicate how close you are to passing the exam and when you may be ready to book your test.

We think that this book is most effective when used in combination with other revision materials and resources. Practice tests are a really good way to monitor progress and determine which topic areas you still need to work on, they aren't as effective at helping you to learn methods and new content. This is why we think that this book should be used in conjunction with other revision materials that help you to learn the areas of each test that you are not confident with as well as online practice tests so that you can become comfortable with the computerised format of the actual exams.

For revision guides, study books and online practice tests please visit www.qtsmathstutor.co.uk.

When using this book please keep in mind the pass mark which are reported to be 63% for both tests. However, we do know that the pass marks can vary slightly depending on the difficulty of the exam so please do not rely on 63% as a guaranteed pass.

About the authors

The QTS Maths and Literacy Tutor team have come together to produce the first QTS practice test book to help prospective teachers prepare for their professional skills tests. Our team of QTS specialists is composed of tutors, qualified teachers and industry experts, all whom have years of experience helping people to pass their professional skills tests.

About this book

This QTS skills test book is one in a series of books aimed at helping prospective teachers prepare for their professional skills tests. This QTS book presents realistic practice tests that give people an insight into the topics and types of questions that may appear in the professional skills exams. The book contains 4 numeracy skills tests and 4 literacy skills tests with corresponding answers, so you can easily check which questions you have answered correctly whilst determining the areas you need to work on. Both sets of practice tests follow the same structure as the actual exam. The literacy tests cover spelling, punctuation, grammar and comprehension; whilst the numeracy tests contain all the major topics covered in the exam. Both sets of tests have an answers section, but they do not contain detailed solutions or explanations.

The tests within this book are a good form of practise for both of your professional skills tests but we do strongly recommend that the tests are used in combination with online practice tests that provide a test format more closely aligned with the real exams which are carried out on computers. To access a free online numeracy and literacy test please visit www.qtsmathstutor.co.uk.

About the Numeracy Skills Test

The numeracy skills test comprises of two sections, a mental arithmetic section followed by a written data section. The 12 mental arithmetic questions require you to calculate your answers within 18 seconds of the second repeat of the question. You must answer all 12 questions in a row and there is no option to go back. You are not permitted to use a calculator in this part of the test.

The written section is made up of 16 onscreen graph and data questions. You have a total of 36 minutes to answer questions 13 to 28 which are based on graphs, tables and data interpretation. You are permitted to use an onscreen calculator in this part of the test.

Both sections of the test require you to submit your answer onscreen, very similar to the QTS Maths Tutor interactive tests and the government practice tests which you can find online using the website links below. Many people ask, what is the pass mark for the numeracy skills test? The answer is it changes depending on the difficulty of the test. The average pass mark appears to be around 18, or 63%. Whilst doing the practice numeracy skills tests, we advise that you aim to achieve 20 or more to be confident in passing the real exam.

There is more information about the skills tests, common mistakes, testing centres and much more at: **www.QTSMathsTutor.co.uk** and **http://sta.education.gov.uk/**.

About the Literacy Skills Test

The QTS literacy test is divided into four sections: spelling, punctuation, grammar and reading comprehension. Unless you have special arrangements, you have 45 minutes to complete the test. The total number of marks available in the test is between 45 and 49 and is broken down as follows:

Spelling – 10 marks

Punctuation – 15 marks

Grammar – 10 – 12 marks

Reading Comprehension - 10 – 12 marks

The pass mark of the test does vary slightly according to the difficulty of the test but is normally set around the 65% mark.

The spelling section is the only part of the test which you cannot revisit once you have submitted your answers. You can review your answers in the other three sections, meaning that if you are struggling with a given question, you can flag it, move on, and come back to it later, time permitting of course.

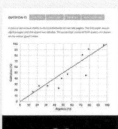
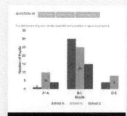

9

Numeracy test 1

Mental arithmetic section (non-calculator)

1. The table tennis room in the school is 8.4 metres long and 4.6 metres wide. What is the area of the table tennis room in metres squared?

2. A head of department needs to order 36 exercise books per class. If there are 7 classes and the cost of an exercise book is 20 pence, what is the total cost of the order? Give your answer in pounds and pence.

3. What is 5.2 – 0.7?

4. A teacher earns £26,000 and receives a 1% pay rise. What is the teacher's new salary?

5. An entrance fee to a Spanish water park is 26 euros. If the exchange rate is 1.3 euros to the pound, how much is the entrance fee in pounds?

6. A teacher left her house at 8:50 to go to a conference. The journey to the conference took 45 minutes. If the teacher spent 3 hours and 50 minutes at the conference, at what time did she arrive back home? Give your answer using the 24 hour clock.

7. A table is 5m metres long. If a coin has a diameter of 0.5 centimetres, how many coins can be placed side by side on the table?

8. 60% of a class have reading difficulties. If there are 35 children in the class, how many children do not have reading difficulties?

9. A pupil who is 11 years and 7 months old has a spelling age of 16 years and 2 months. What is the difference between this pupil's spelling age and actual age in years and months?

10. What is 37.5% of 32 metres?

11. To make 18 cakes, a recipe needs 1.5 kilograms of flour. How many grams of flour are needed to make 6 cakes?

12. 24 pupils are asked to bring in £1.25 for charity. What is the total amount collected?

Written data section (calculator allowed)

13. The English department are planning to take the year 10 students to see the play 'Warhorse'. The ratio of teachers to students is 1:8. If there is a total of 27 people going on the trip, what is the total cost of all the tickets if they are priced as follows:

Ticket type	Ticket price
Adult	£12.50
Student	£8.75

14. A student is sponsored to cycle a distance of 2000 kilometres during the month of August. On the 9th of August, he cycles 35 miles which takes his total for the month to 400 miles. How many more kilometres does he need to cycle on average per day for the remainder of the month. Use the approximation that 5 miles is the equivalent of 8km and give your answer to one decimal place.

15. Here are the results of two separate mock examination tests for a year 11 group, one from January, and another in March.

Student name	January mock	March mock
Billy	46	51
Sue	38	41
Gary	62	70
Gemma	47	48
Reuben	55	59
Lisa	26	32
Libby	35	43

What proportion of students made at least a 10% improvement in their test scores? Give your answer as a fraction in its simplest form.

16. A school is divided into 5 Houses. The table below shows the participation, by House, in the school's Duke of Edinburgh programme.

House	Duke of Edinburgh participants	Total students in House
Mozart	36	85
Debussy	32	92
Bach	39	81
Beethoven	58	78
Brahms	45	72

What percentage of the whole school participated in the Duke of Edinburgh programme? Give your answer to the nearest whole number.

17. Four pupils each sat a mathematics test. Based on their level of ability, the pupils either sat a foundation or higher level paper.

Pupil	Tier	Total marks
A	Foundation	38
B	Higher	65
C	Higher	43
D	Foundation	35

Total marks available

Foundation – 45 marks

Higher – 80 marks

Which pupil had the highest percentage mark?

18. A class of students took a test and the scores were recorded in a frequency table. What was the mean test score? Give your answer to the nearest whole number.

Test score out of 10	Number of students
6	12
7	8
8	6
9	6
10	3

19. Following a spelling test, a teacher tracked her class of 15 students by comparing their spelling age to their actual age on a scatter graph.

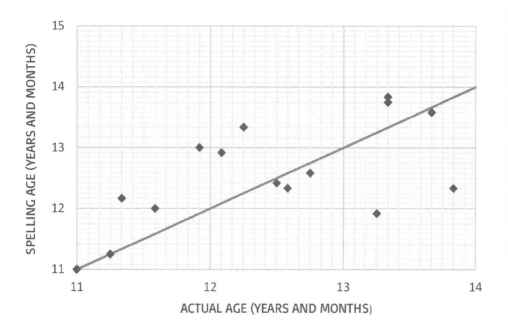

Which of the following statements are true?

a. 1/3 of the students had a spelling age that was less than their actual age.

b. There were two students who had a spelling age of 13 years and 4 months.

c. The greatest difference between spelling age and actual age was 1 year and 4 months.

20. Following a spelling test, a teacher tracked her class of 15 students by comparing their spelling age to their actual age on a scatter graph.

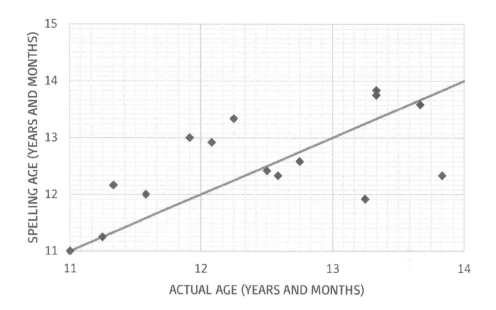

What was the median actual age in this class?

21. A school tracked its maths, English and science mock exam results, and the data was plotted using box and whisker diagrams.

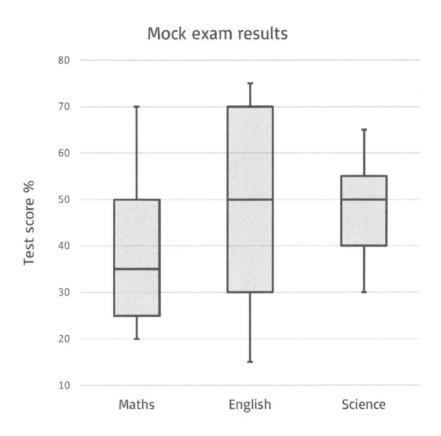

Mock exam results

Which of the following statements are true? Tick all that apply.

a) English was the subject with the greatest range of results.
b) The interquartile range of English results was greater than the overall range of science results.
c) 3/4 of the maths students scored more than the median score for English.

22. 4 schools conducted mock 11 plus tests and the data was plotted using box and whisker diagrams.

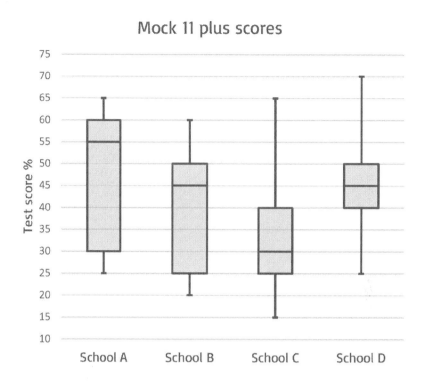

Mock 11 plus scores

Which of the following statements are true? Tick all that apply.

a) School D had the highest median score.
b) The greatest range was in school C.
c) 25% of the students in school C scored less than the lowest mark in school D.

23. The below bar chart shows how many students achieved grades 7, 8 and 9 for English, Maths and French in a school.

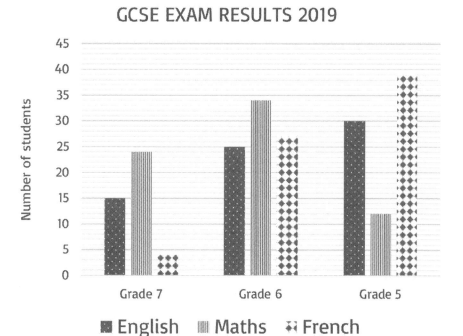

What was the difference between the number of students who achieved a grade 5 and a grade 7 in maths?

24. The below scatter graph charts scores for 13 students for a literacy and a numeracy test.

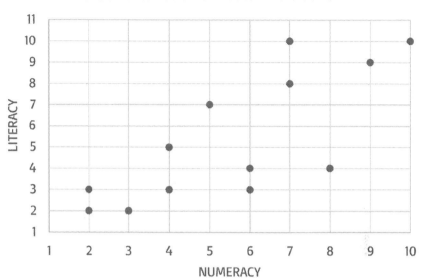

YEAR 6 NUMERACY AND LITERACY

What was the median score for numeracy?

25. The below scatter graph charts scores for 13 students for a literacy and a numeracy test.

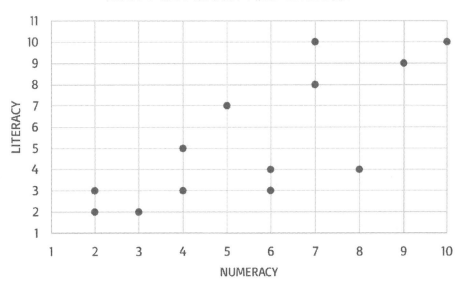

YEAR 6 NUMERACY AND LITERACY

What percentage of the students achieved the same score for both numeracy and literacy? Give your answer to the nearest percentage.

26. The below cumulative frequency graph shows the performance of some students in a recent SATS test.

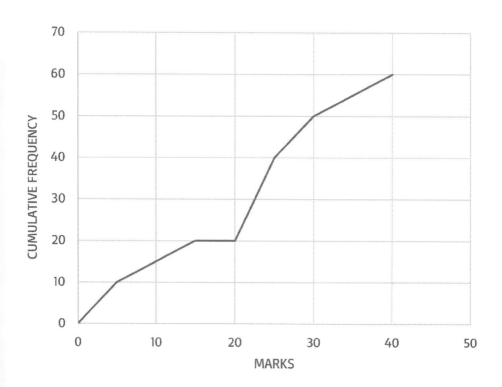

Which of the following statements are true?

    a) Not a single student scored between 15 and 20 marks.
    b) There was a total of 60 students.
    c) The median score was 30 marks.

27. The below bar graph shows the number of negatives received per form group.

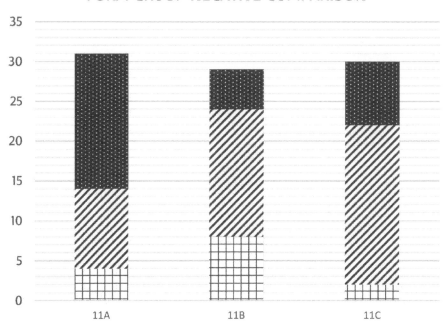

FORM GROUP NEGATIVE COMPARISON

+ 1 - 10 negatives ⬛ 10 - 30 negatives ⬛ Over 30 negatives

How many students in total scored between 10 and 30 negatives?

28. 6 students take 4 separate tests. A raw score is formed which is the sum of these 4 tests. This raw score is referenced against the pupils' age so that standardised scores are obtained for each student.

		Age in years and months				
		8,0	8,1	8,2	8,3	8,4
Raw data	181 – 190	100	90	80	70	60
	171 – 180	110	100	90	80	70
	161 – 170	120	110	100	90	80
	151 – 160	130	120	110	100	90
	140 – 150	140	130	120	110	100

Student	Test A	Test B	Test C	Test D	Age (years and months)
A	36	32	38	40	8y 4m
B	41	42	35	39	8y 2m
C	43	44	44	46	8y 3m
D	50	36	36	41	8y 4m
E	42	43	43	39	8y 1m
F	48	46	45	42	8y 3m

What proportion of the students achieved a score of more than 100? Give your answer as a percentage to the nearest whole number.

Numeracy test 2

Mental arithmetic section (non-calculator)

1. A teacher travels at a speed of 40 kilometres per hour and travels 180 kilometres. How long does the journey take in hours and minutes?

2. What is 425 ÷ 0.5?

3. At an INSET day, 2 hours and 40 minutes was dedicated to behaviour management and then there was a 1 hour and 10 minute break, and the remainder of the session was about differentiation. If the INSET day lasted 5 hours and 20 minutes, how long was the session on differentiation? Give your answer in hours and minutes.

4. In a year group of 105 children, 2/7 study French. How many students do not study French?

5. In the recent sports day, the school's previous 60 metre record of 11.4 seconds was beaten by 0.8 seconds. What is the new 100 metre record?

6. 40 students go on a trip. The trip costs £16.50 per student. What is the combined cost for the 40 students?

7. The oldest student in a class is 10 years and 4 months and the youngest is 9 years and 5 months. What is the age difference between these two students?

8. A school day starts at 8:25. There are 6 lessons that last 50 minutes each. There is a morning break of 15 minutes and a lunchtime break of 1 hour. What time does the school day end? Give your answer using the 24 hour clock.

9. Pupils receiving free school meals are entitled to a food allowance of £2.85 per school day. What is their food allowance per week?

10. A student scores 14/20, 14/20, 16/20 and 8/20 in 4 separate French tests. What is the student's mean test score?

11. Coaches seat 15 people. On a school trip, the ratio of adults to children is 1:8. If there are 42 children on the trip, how many coaches are needed?

12. 200 students are in year 11. 62% passed the mock English GCSE exam in February but in the actual GCSE in June, 73% secured a pass. How many students who failed the mock exam in February managed to pass the actual GCSE in June?

Written data section (calculator allowed)

13. A trainee teacher has a job interview that starts at 10:30. She would like to arrive at the school at least 40 minutes before the start of the interview in order to revise potential interview questions. If the teacher lives 180 miles away and estimates that she will travel at an average speed of 80 kilometres per hour, what is the latest time that she should leave home? Use the approximation that 5 miles is the equivalent of 8 kilometres.

14. The exchange rates between 3 currencies are displayed below:

| 1 British pound = 1.34 US dollars |
| 1 US dollar = 1.39 Australian dollars |

How many Australian dollars will you get if you are exchanging 240 British pounds? Give your answer to the nearest dollar.

15. A teacher needs to make a purchase of 1000 colouring pencils for an art project.   What is the difference in prices between the two companies?

Company type	Number of pencils in pack	Cost per pack	Offer	Postage
Internet company	20	£1.50	5 for 4	£4.25
Mail order stationery company	25	£1.90	4 for 3	£6.99

16. A tutor records the marks achieved by his 6 students in two test papers. Each student sat the same two papers. The tutor enters the number of questions that the students answered correctly into the table below.

	Test 1	Test 2
Pupil 1	12	17
Pupil 2	16	14
Pupil 3	7	12
Pupil 4	14	15
Pupil 5	18	14
Pupil 6	5	7

What is the percentage increase in the total number of marks achieved across all pupils combined in test 2 from the number of marks achieved across all pupils combined in test 1? Give your answer correct to one decimal place.

17. The table below displays the percentage marks that three pupils achieved who sat the same two exam papers.

Student	Paper 1		Paper 2	
	Mark	Weighting	Mark	Weighting
A	66	0.3	84	0.5
B	72	0.3	78	0.5
C	57	0.3	90	0.5

Final mark = (paper 1 mark x paper 1 weighting) + (paper 2 mark x paper 1 weighting)

What is the mean final mark across the three students?

18. Using the formula $\frac{(4a+b)}{3}$ = overall test score, what was a student's score for test B if he scored 12 in test A and had an overall test score of 80?

19. Following a reading test, a teacher tracked her class of 21 students by comparing their reading age to their actual age on a scatter graph.

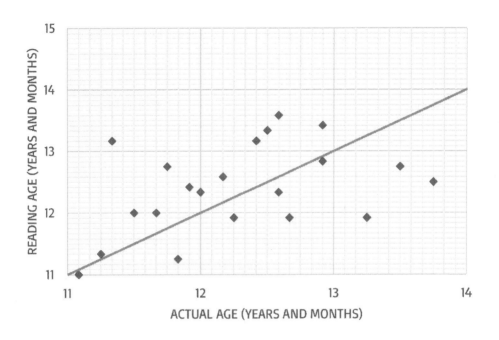

Which of the following statements are true?

    a) 3 students had a reading age that was the same as their actual age.
    b) The students aged between 11 and 12 performed better in the test relative to their age than the students aged between 13 and 14.
    c) 3/7 of the class had a reading age that was lower than their actual age.

20. Following a reading test, a teacher tracked her class of 21 students by comparing their reading age to their actual age on a scatter graph.

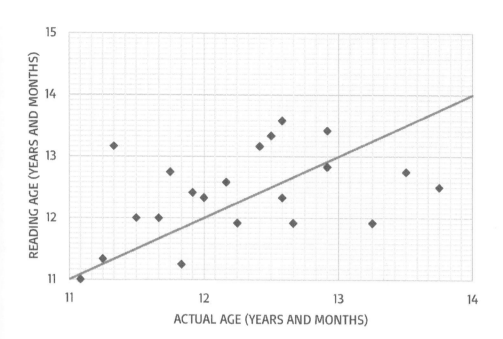

What was the median reading age?

21. Two classes completed a physics mock exam and the data was plotted using box and whisker diagrams.

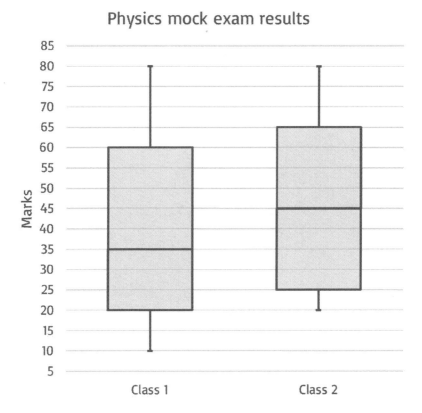

Physics mock exam results

Which of the following statements are true? Tick all that apply.

a) The median mark for class 2 was 10 marks higher than the median for class 1.

b) 3/4 of class 1 scored 20 marks or more.

c) In class 2, the number of students who scored between 20 and 25 marks was the same as the number of students who scored between 25 and 45 marks.

22. The below bar chart shows how lesson observations were graded over a three-year period.

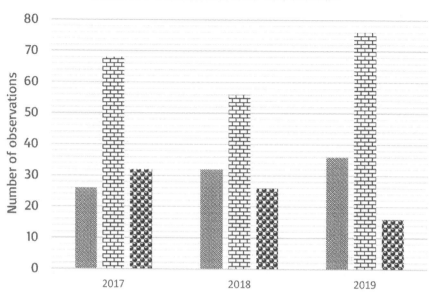

LESSON OBSERVATION GRADINGS

■ Outstanding   ╪ Good   ✖ Requires improvement

Which of the following statements are true?

a) There was a continued increase in the number of outstanding lessons between 2017 and 2019.

b) There was a 50% decrease in the number of lessons requiring improvement between 2017 and 2019.

c) The number of outstanding lessons between 2017 and 2019 increased by 10%.

23. 12 students took a test in both English and maths and their results were plotted on the below scatter graph.

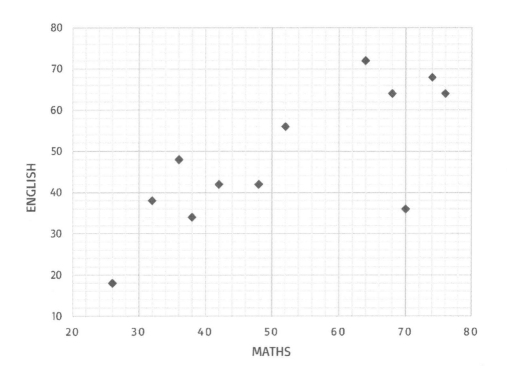

What was the difference between the range for English and the range for maths?

24. 12 students took a test in both English and maths and their results were plotted on the below scatter graph.

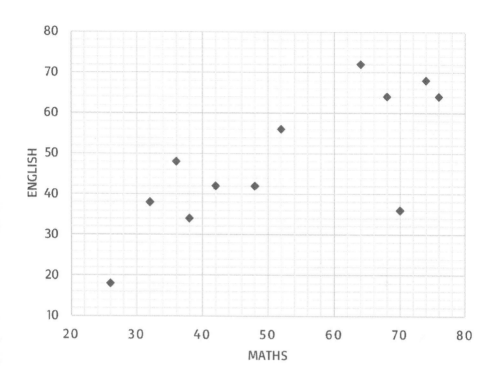

What was the median score for English?

25. The below cumulative frequency graph shows the performance of some students in a recent mock 11 plus test.

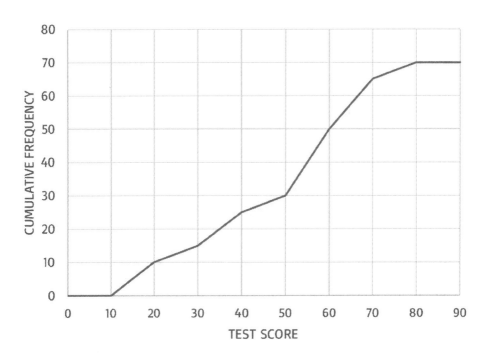

Which of the following statements are true?

  a) 20 students scored between 50 and 60 marks.
  b) Not a single student scored less than 10.
  c) 30 students scored 50 or above.

26. The below bar graph shows how lessons were graded within a school over a three-year period.

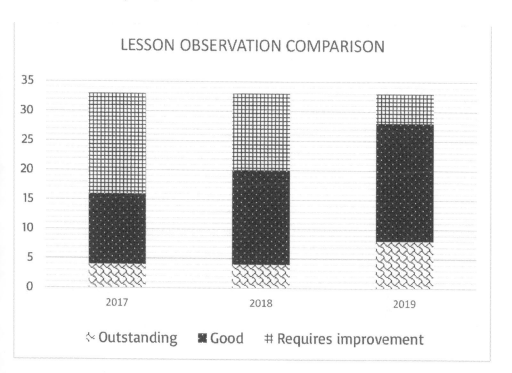

What was the percentage decrease in the number of lessons that required improvement between 2017 and 2019? Give your answer to the nearest whole number.

27. The below pie charts show a comparison of two schools and how their free school meals students are broken down by year group.

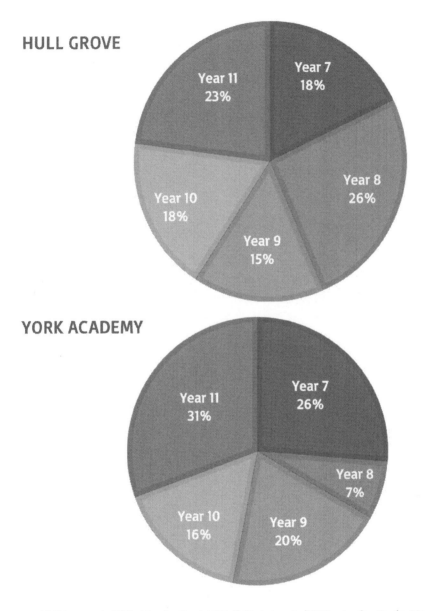

HULL GROVE

Year 11
23%

Year 7
18%

Year 8
26%

Year 10
18%

Year 9
15%

YORK ACADEMY

Year 11
31%

Year 7
26%

Year 8
7%

Year 10
16%

Year 9
20%

If there are 179 students in Hull Grove and 213 students in York Academy, what is the difference between the number of students in year 7 who receive free school meals? Give your answer to the nearest whole number.

28. For the year 7 Valentine's Day dance, the head of year plans to use the school hall. As part of the entertainment, part of the school hall will be set aside for a small stage for the student band to perform. The area of the hall and the area of the stage is shown in the below diagram. What is the area of hall in metres squared which wiii be available for dancing?

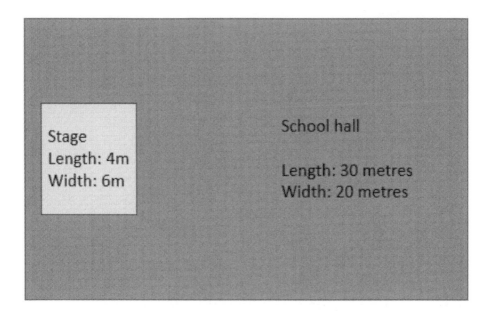

Stage
Length: 4m
Width: 6m

School hall

Length: 30 metres
Width: 20 metres

Numeracy test 3

Mental arithmetic section (non-calculator)

1. What is 212 divided by 0.2?

2. In a group of 25 music students, 12 play the guitar. What percentage of music students play the guitar?

3. Gary and Fred share £60 in the ratio of 3:2. How much does Gary receive?

4. A teacher buys 12 pens and 10 pencils. Pens cost 16 pence each and pencils are 14 pence each. Calculate the total cost of the order. Give your answer in pounds and pence.

5. Assuming that 5 miles is approximately the equivalent of 8 kilometres, what is 72 kilometres in miles?

6. 12 students have a total of 192 house points between them. What is the mean number of house points that each student has?

7. A teacher travels 42 kilometres to school. Petrol costs approximately 11 pence per kilometre. How much does the teacher spend per school week on petrol?

8. What is 62.5% of 48?

9. A teacher buys 32 exercise books at a cost of 25 pence each and 1 ruler costing 75 pence. How much change does she receive from a £20 note?

10. A parents evening starts at 4:15. A teacher sees 15 parents for 8 minutes each and has a 20 minute break. What time does the teacher finish? Give your answer using the 24 hour clock.

11. Out of 160 students, 3/5 plan to go to university. How many students do not plan to go to university?

12. What is 36% of 250?

Written data section (calculator allowed)

13. A teaching agency is planning a training day which consists of a series of educational lectures for supply staff. The first session on behaviour management lasts for 1 hour and 25 minutes, the second on teaching and learning lasts for 1 hour and 10 minutes, and the third on differentiation lasts for 1 hour and 40 minutes. There is a short break of 15 minutes between sessions 1 and 2 and a lunch break of 30 minutes. If the training day starts at 8.45, what time does the training day finish?

14. An ICT teacher wishes to buy some new computer monitors.

Company	Price per monitor	Promotion
A	£160	4 for the price of 3
B	£150	20% discount

What is the difference in price, between company A and B, if the ICT teacher plans to buy 30 monitors in total?

15. The head of year 11 analysed the year group's GCSE results by form.

Form group	Number of children in class	Number of children achieving 5 GCSEs
11A	28	21
11B	26	20
11C	30	18
11D	32	26
11E	31	24
11F	25	15

Which of the following statements are true? Tick all that apply.

a) The percentage of students in 11C achieving 5 GCSE passes is the same as the percentage of students in 11F.

b) The form group with the greatest percentage of students achieving 5 GCSE passes was 11D.

c) 1/3 of the students in 11A did not achieve 5 GCSEs.

16. What is the mean number of books read in this class of 43 students? Give your answer correct to the nearest whole number.

Number of books read	Number of students
1 book	16
2 books	12
3 books	8
4 books	4
5 books	3

17. Using the formula $\dfrac{a+3b}{5}$ = overall test score, what was a student's score for test B if he scored 20 in test A and had an overall test score of 64?

18. A teacher compared the initial test results of six of her pupils to their resit marks. The marks are shown in the table below.

Student	Initial mark	Resit mark
A	25	35
B	30	40
C	45	60
D	35	42
E	50	70
F	26	32

Which student saw a 20% increase in their resit mark from their original mark?

19. Following a spelling test, a teacher tracked her class of 25 students by comparing their spelling age to their actual age on a scatter graph.

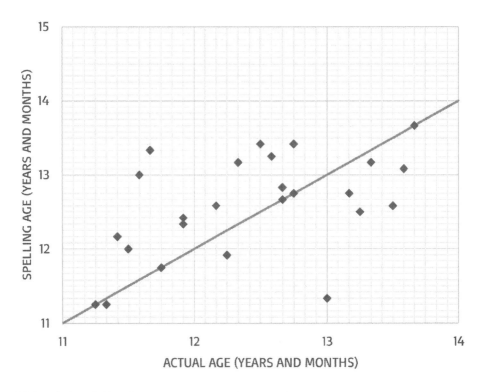

Which of the following statements are true?

a) 25% of the class had a spelling age that was the same as their actual age.

b) The student who had the best spelling age compared to actual age was 11 years and 8 months old.

c) Not a single student aged 13 or over had a spelling age that was better than their age.

20. Following a spelling test, a teacher tracked her class of 25 students by comparing their spelling age to their actual age on a scatter graph.

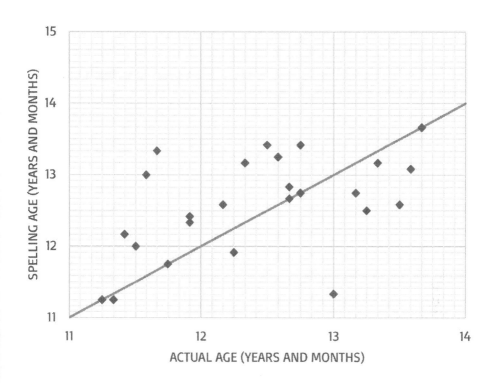

What percentage of the class had a spelling age which was more than 13 years?

21. Two classes completed a spelling test and the data was plotted using box and whisker diagrams.

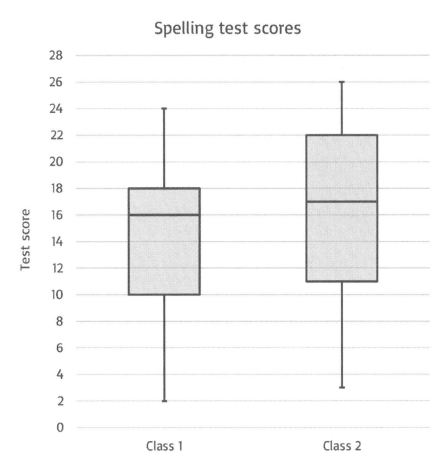

Spelling test scores

Which of the following statements are true? Tick all that apply.

a) The median test score was the same for both classes.

b) In class 1, the number of students who scored between 10 and 16 marks was the same as the number of students who scored between 16 and 18 marks.

c) Class 2 had the greater range.

22. A school's humanities department tracked its history and geography scores and the data was plotted using box and whisker diagrams.

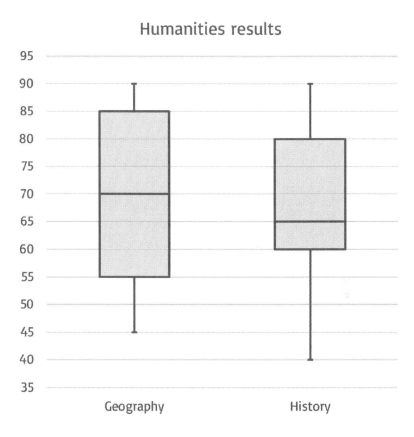

Humanities results

Which of the following statements are true? Tick all that apply.

a) Fewer students scored above 85 in geography than scored above 80 in history.

b) There was a difference of 5 between the range in history and geography.

c) 50% of the history students scored more than 65.

23. The below bar graph compares male and female student performance in a maths GCSE.

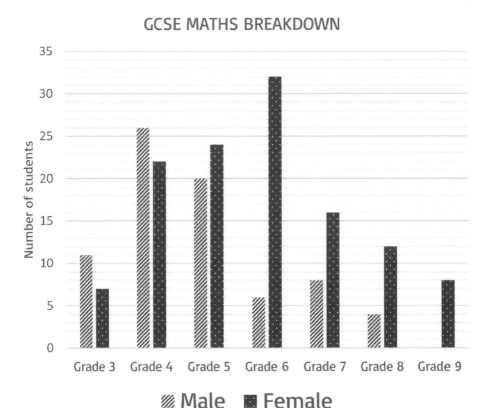

GCSE MATHS BREAKDOWN

Which of the following statements are true?

a) The modal grade for the female students was a grade 6.
b) The number of male students achieving a grade 7 was the same as the number of female students achieving a grade 9.
c) 50% more male students achieved a grade 4 than a grade 3.

24. 10 students took a test in French and Spanish and the results were plotted on a scatter graph.

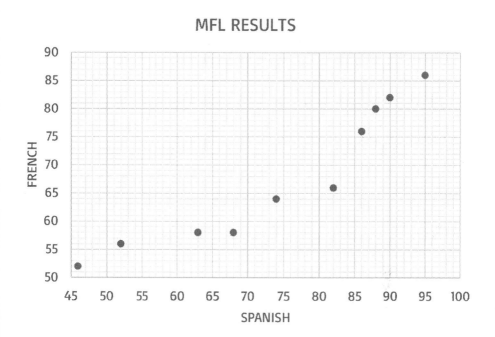

MFL RESULTS

What was the proportion of students who performed better in French than Spanish? Give your answer as a fraction in its simplest form.

25. 10 students took a test in French and Spanish and the results were plotted on a scatter graph.

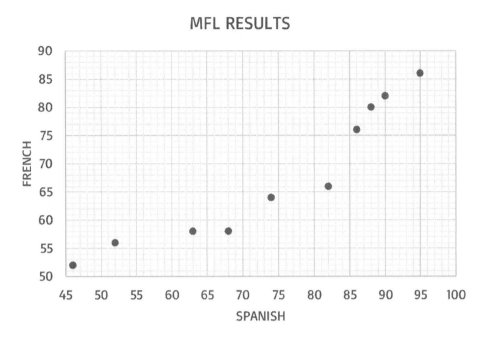

MFL RESULTS

What was the median score for French?

26. The below cumulative frequency graph shows the performance of some students in a GCSE art exam.

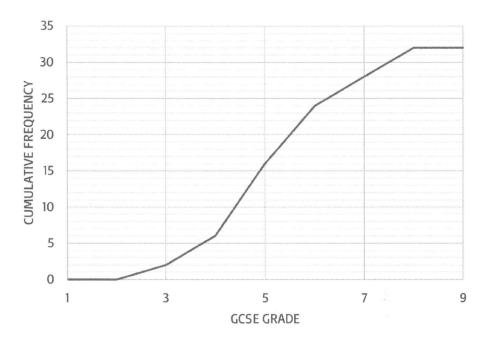

Which of the following statements are true?

    a) The median grade was 5.
    b) 5 students achieved a level 4 or below.
    c) 32 students achieved a grade 9.

27. The below bar graph shows how many detentions three students, Reece, Gary and Steve received over a three-year period.

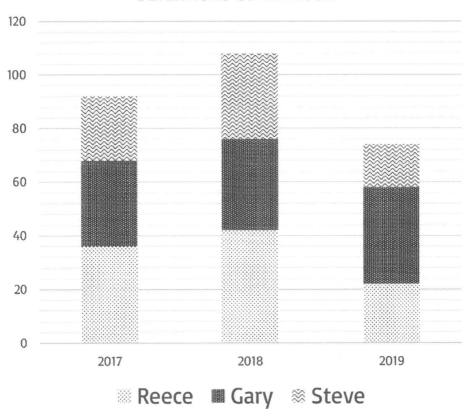

DETENTIONS COMPARISON

Reece ■ Gary Steve

What was the percentage increase in the number of detentions Steve received from 2017 to 2018? Give your answer to the nearest whole number.

28. The headteacher of school A is comparing his GCSE results to school B. In school A there are 170 students while there are 132 in school B.

SCHOOL A

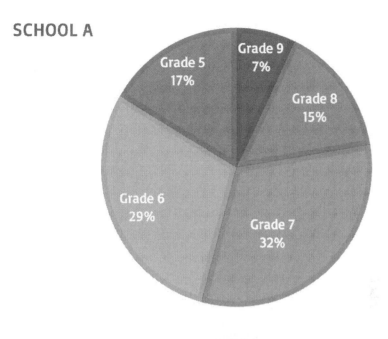

SCHOOL B

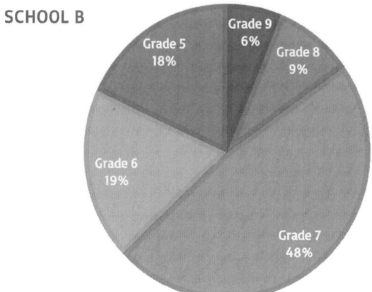

What was the difference between the number of students who achieved a grade 7 in both schools? Give your answer to the nearest whole number.

Numeracy test 4

Mental arithmetic section (non-calculator)

1. What is 55% of 160?

2. How many parents evening appointments can a teacher fit in if each appointment is 8 minutes long and the parents evening lasts for 3 hours?

3. 9 out of 60 students dropped French at the end of year 9. What percentage of students did not drop French at the end of year 9?

4. In a class of 40 students, 1/4 study French and 1/8 study German. The remainder study Spanish. How many students study Spanish?

5. What is 64 ÷ 0.2?

6. A teacher needs to order 134 exercise books which cost 25 pence each. How much is the total order? Give your answer in pounds and pence.

7. A teacher wants to change £25 into Australian dollars. If the exchange rate is £1 = AUS$1.80, how many dollars does she receive?

8. The length of a table is 3m. A child wants to see how many coins fit side by side across the length of the table. If each coin has a diameter of 2cm, how many coins can the child fit along the length of the table?

9. A teacher earns £32,000 and receives a 4% pay increase. What is her new salary?

10. In a class of 36 students, 24 have had their immunisations. What fraction of the students have not had their immunisations?

11. 40 pupils were doing a sponsored swim and swam 10 lengths each. If they were sponsored 25p per length, how much did they raise in total? Give your answer in pounds.

12. A lesson starts at 2:35pm. There is a starter activity that lasts 10 minutes, a written task that takes 35 minutes and then a peer assessment task which takes a further 10 minutes. What time does the lesson end? Give your answer using the 24 hour clock.

Written data section (calculator allowed)

13. A teacher is going on a geography field trip to Swanage with 12 students. The trip will involve staying in a youth hostel for 3 nights. The total of the accommodation for all 12 students for the 3 nights is £288. The teacher estimates that the trip from the school in Birmingham to Swanage is about 160 miles. A litre of petrol costs £1.19 and it is estimated that the minibus has a fuel economy of 10 miles per litre. The teacher plans to charge the students for accommodation and fuel, so how much does he need to charge each student? Give your answer to the nearest pound.

14. A form tutor is looking at the number of detentions received by students in his form group for the previous half term.

Number of detentions	Frequency
0	5
1	3
2	7
3	4
4	2
5	3
6	2
7	1
8	2

Calculate the mean number of detentions per student.

15. The table below shows the participation in sports activities by year group.

Year group	Students who represent the school for sport	Total students in year group
Year 7	140	204
Year 8	102	178
Year 9	86	168
Year 10	68	162
Year 11	45	145

What percentage of the whole school represented the school for sport? Give your answer to the nearest whole number.

16. An ICT teacher wants to buy 60 new keyboards for the school's ICT suites. He has three different online retailers to choose from, each offering different deals.

Retailer	Cost per item	Offer	Delivery total
A	£6.25	5 for the price of 4	£9.80
B	£7.60	3 for the price of 2	£8.60
C	£5.95	20% off each item	£25

What is the difference between the most expensive and least expensive company?

17. What is the mean number of lengths swam by this class of 40 students? Give your answer to the nearest number of lengths.

Lengths swam	Number of students
6 lengths	8
8 lengths	6
10 lengths	4
12 lengths	10
14 lengths	12

18. Following a reading test, a teacher tracked her class of 27 students by comparing their reading age to their actual age on a scatter graph.

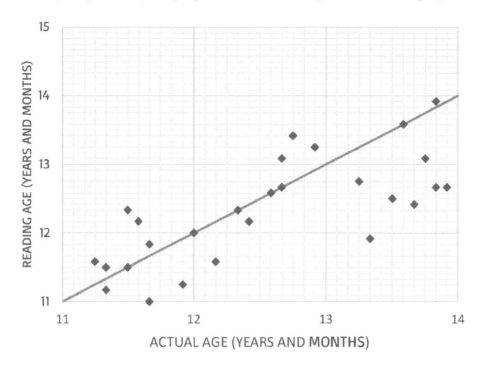

Which of the following statements are true?

    a. 2/9 of the class had a reading age that was the same as their actual age.

    b. The proportion of the class who have a more advanced reading age compared to actual age is greater than the proportion of the class who have a less advanced reading age compared to actual age.

    c. The median actual age in this class is 12 years and 11 months.

19. Following a reading test, a teacher tracked her class of 27 students by comparing their reading age to their actual age on a scatter graph.

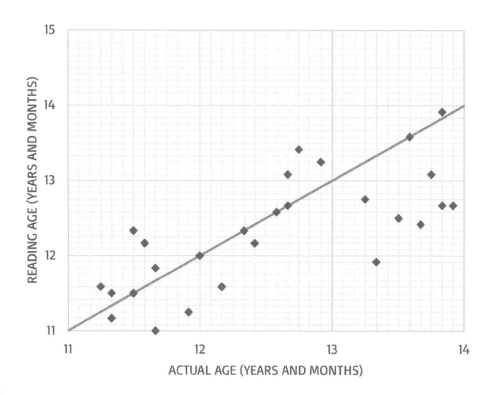

Circle the student whose has the best reading age compared to actual age.

20. A modern languages department conducted progress tests for their students and the data was plotted using box and whisker diagrams. Both classes were made up of 30 students.

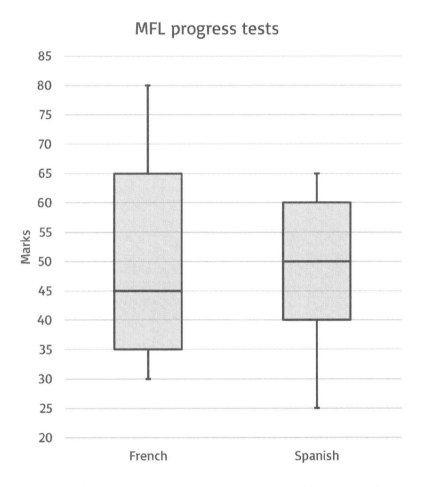

Which of the following statements are true? Tick all that apply.

   a) There was a difference of 10 marks between the median scores for French and Spanish

   b) The range for French was 15 marks more than the range for Spanish.

   c) 15 students scored 45 marks or more in the French test.

21. Mr McGoldrick and Mr Wright both conducted end of year tests with their classes and the data was plotted using box and whisker diagrams.

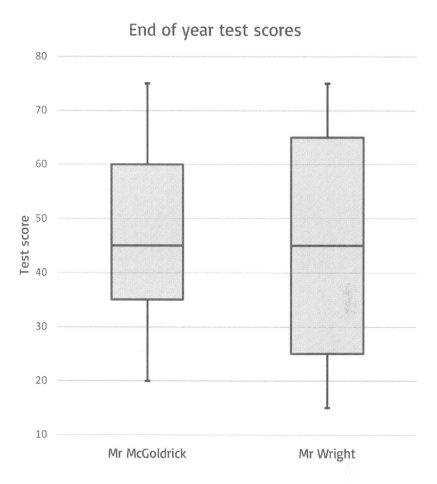

End of year test scores

Which of the following statements are true? Tick all that apply.

a) The median score for both classes was the same.
b) The interquartile range for Mr McGoldrick's class was greater than the interquartile range for Mr Wright's class.
c) In Mr McGoldrick's class, 25% of pupils scored more than 60.

22. The below graph shows a breakdown of the number of students per House (Shackleton, Adam, Turner and Brunel) who received between 0 – 10 negatives, 11 – 20 negatives, 21 – 30 negatives and more than 30 negatives.

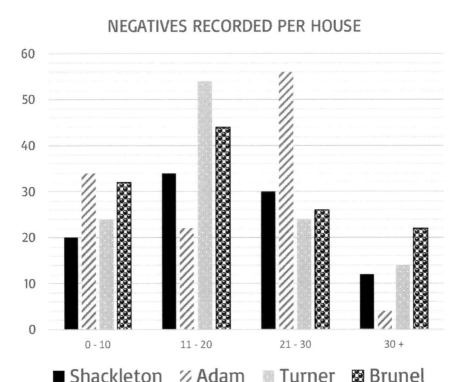

NEGATIVES RECORDED PER HOUSE

Which of the following statements are true?

a) 50% more students in Shackleton House received between 11 and 20 negatives than between 0 and 10 negatives.
b) The number of students in Adam House receiving between 11 and 20 negatives was the same as the number of students in Brunel House who received over 30 negatives.
c) The modal number of negatives was 11 – 20.

23. 12 students sat two maths papers, paper 1 and paper 2, and their results were plotted on as a scatter graph.

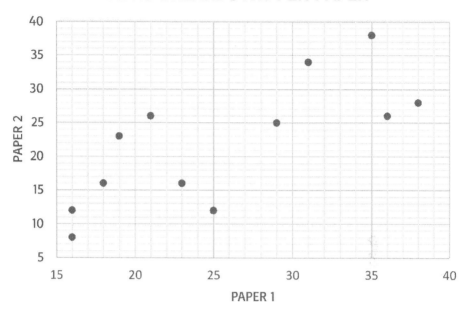

What proportion of the group performed better in paper 1? Give your answer as a fraction in its simplest form.

24. 12 students sat two maths papers, paper 1 and paper 2, and their results were plotted on as a scatter graph.

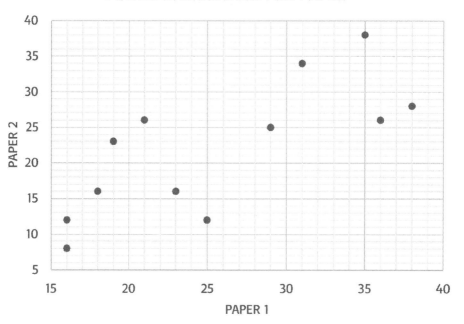

MATHS BREAKDOWN PER PAPER

What was the range for paper 2?

25. The below cumulative frequency graph shows the performance of some students in a maths test.

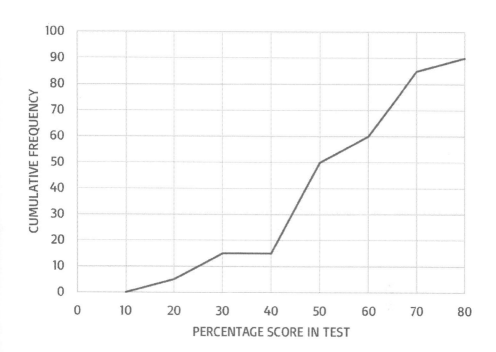

Which of the following statements are true?

a) Not a single student scored less than 10%.
b) Approximately 15 students scored between 30% and 40%.
c) 30 students scored over 60%.

26. The below bar graph shows the number of students who achieved 5 or more GCSE passes over a three-year period.

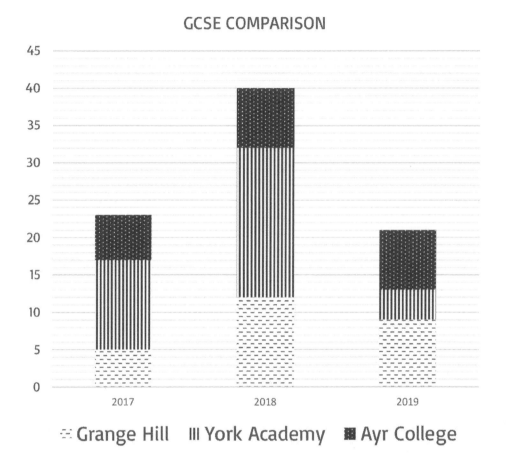

GCSE COMPARISON

⋯ Grange Hill   ⦙⦙⦙ York Academy   ▓ Ayr College

Which school showed the biggest percentage increase from 2017 to 2018?

27. 5 students take 4 separate tests. A raw score is formed which is the sum of these 4 tests. This raw score is referenced against the pupils' age so that standardised scores are obtained for each student.

		Age in years and months				
		8,0	8,1	8,2	8,3	8,4
Raw data	271 – 275	81	79	77	75	73
	266 – 270	83	81	79	77	75
	261 – 265	85	83	81	79	77
	256 – 260	87	85	83	81	79
	251 – 255	89	87	85	83	81

Student	Test A	Test B	Test C	Test D	Age (years and months)
Bob	65	63	66	69	8y 3m
Gary	63	64	62	67	8y 1m
Belinda	66	65	67	70	8y 0m
Wayne	66	66	67	65	8y 4m
Susan	62	61	65	65	8y 3m

What proportion of the students achieved a score of more than 80? Give your answer as a percentage?

28. The head of maths is comparing the recent set of GCSE grades to the previous year. There were 97 students in total in 2018, whereas there were 104 in 2019. How many more students achieved a grade 4 in 2019? Give your answer to the nearest whole number.

2018

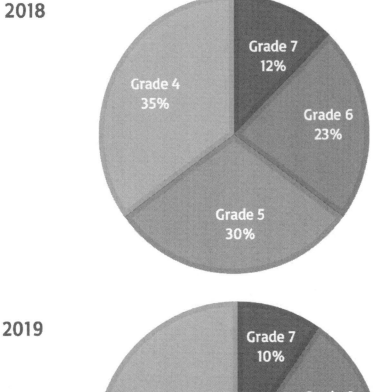

2019

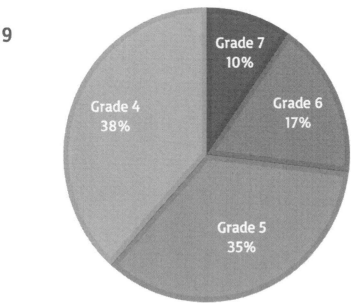

QTS LITERACY TUTOR
WWW.LITERACYSKILLSTEST.CO.UK

 Based on hundreds of reviews on

FREE ONLINE LITERACY SKILLS TEST
EXPERT 1 TO 1 TUITION WITH OUR QTS SPECIALISTS

WHAT QTS LITERACY TUTOR HAS TO OFFER

Spelling Practice

Punctuation Questions

Grammar Section

Comprehension Resources

Practice Tests

Expert Tutors

Correct Format

New Question Formats

Visit www.literacyskillstest.co.uk to take a Free Full Practice Test today.

10
LITERACY SKILLS TESTS

97%
LEARNER PASS RATE

490
TEST QUESTIONS

68

Literacy test 1 (47 marks)

Spelling (10 marks)

1. The   PGCE   mentor   highlighted   the   lack   of
    _____ in   the   lesson   observation.
    (differentiation / diferentiation / differrentiation / differenciation)

2. Mr Barlow is the _____ officer for the union.
    (liason / liaison / laison / liasion)

3. It is not _____ for teachers to leave their
    students unattended at any time. (acceptable / acceptible /
    aceptible / acseptable)

4. The new student in the class seems to be attracting for too much
    _____ attention.   (unecessary / unecesary /
    uneccessary / unnecessary)

5. I would not agree that _____ is a problem in
    this school. (disipline / disciplin / disiplin / discipline)

6. Since students routinely forget _____, the
    school will provide spare equipment during the exams. (stationary
    / stationery / stationairy / stationiery)

7. The fact that the school is now in special measures is a source of
    _____ to   many   staff   members.
    (embarassment   /   embarrasment   /   embarasment   /
    embarrassment)

8. The student was removed from the chemistry lesson for _____ breaking a set of test tubes. (acidentally / accidentelly / acidentelly / accidentally)

9. Pupils need to know how many years are in a_____ for the upcoming test. (milennium / millenium / millennium / milenium)

10. It is not _____ that George is making much progress in maths. (aparent / apparant / apparent / aparant)

Punctuation (15 marks)

Dear Parent / Carer

Please find enclosed a copy of your childs mock examination results. Students will have received these results in their lessons, but we thought it would be useful and informative for you to receive a copy of all your child's results on one page. The mock examination results exist to give students practice of revision and of sitting formal examinations they are very useful for identifying gaps in knowledge skills to improve, or aspects of examination technique to refine. In order to help you interpret your child's result teachers have been asked to signify whether an examination grade is a cause for concern'. This indicates that a change of approach is needed, and that your child will have to speak immediately with their teacher, and act on the advice they are given in order to improve their grade.

It is possible that your child scored a much lower grade than they are currently being tracked at and hope to achieve) in the real examinations, but this has not been identified as a problem this does not mean that the teacher has lowered his or her expectations for your child, but that the reason for the underperformance is easily fixable.

In your discussions with your child about their mock results please emphasise the key message that the mocks represent the beginning of the revision process and that there is plenty of time before the GCSE take place in may. Your child should look beyond their overall grade in a subject, regardless of whether it is better or worse than expected, and focus on what they need to do to improve next time.

Where you have any queries about an individual subject, please contact the appropriate teacher if you are concerned more broadly about the performance of your child, please contact the Head of Year.

Grammar (10 marks)

Task 1 (3 marks)

In designing the curriculum for the senior school, we aim to give every single child the chance

a) to achieve they're full potential.

b) to achieve their full potential.

c) to fully achieve there potential.

d) to fully achieve they're potential.

We wish our pupils to

a) develop into personable, confident and articulate young adults; develop an inquisitive nature; appreciate the value of learning; and be able to take their place as full, well-informed members of society.

b) develop into personable, confident and articulate young adults; develop an inquisitive nature; appreciating the value of learning; and being able to take their place as full, well-informed members of society.

c) develop into personable, confident and articulate young adults; to develop an inquisitive nature; to appreciate the value of learning; and to be able to take their place as full, well-informed society members.

d) develop into personable, confident and articulate young adults and an inquisitive nature; appreciate the value of learning; and be able to take their place as full, well-informed members of society.

We aim to achieve this

a)   through providing a broad-based, dynamic and stimulating curriculum.

b)   by providing a broad-based, dynamic and stimulating curriculum.

c)   with providing a broad-based, dynamic and stimulating curriculum.

d)   to provide a broad-based, dynamic and stimulating curriculum.

Task 2 (3 marks)

At Grange Hill School, we believe that

a)   all homework must be meaningful, must complement and extend classroom learning, must boost organisational skills and must promote self-discipline and independent learning.

b)   all homework must be meaningful, complementing and extending classroom learning, and must boost organisational skills, promoting self-discipline and independent learning.

c)   all homework must be meaningful, complement and extending classroom learning, boost organisational skills and promote self-discipline and independent learning.

d)   all homework could be meaningful, complement and extend classroom learning, boost organisational skills and to promote self-discipline and independent learning.

Students are

a) encouraged to develop the skills, confidence and motivation needed to study effectively and independently.

b) encouraged to develop the skills, confidence and motivation needed for effectively studying on their own.

c) encouraged to develop the skills, confidence and motivation which are needed to study effectively on their own.

d) encouraged to develop the skills, confidence and motivation that are needed to study effectively and independently.

a) They may be asked to consolidate and reinforce skills and understanding developed in school or extending learning through additional reading.

b) They could be asked to consolidate and reinforce skills and understanding developed in school or to extend learning through additional reading.

c) They could be asked to consolidate and reinforce skills and understanding developed in school or extending learning through additional reading.

d) They may be asked to consolidate and reinforce skills and understanding developed in school or to extend learning through additional reading.

Task 3 (4 marks)

Life as a Sixth Form student is exciting and challenging in many different ways. In the Sixth Form,

a) we are taking great care to ensure that you have all the help that you need to achieve your best.

b) we take great care to insure that you have all the help what you need to achieve your best.

c) we take great care to ensure that you have all the help you need to achieve your best.

d) we take great care to insure that you have all the help that you need in order to settle in and achieve your best.

At interview and enrolment, members of our Sixth Form Team

a) discuss options and choices with you and your personalised study programme will be timetabled around your needs.

b) will discuss options and choices with you and your personalised study programme will be timetabled around your needs.

c) may discuss options and choices with you and your personal study programme will be timetabled around your needs.

d) will discuss options and choices with you and your personalised programme of study will be timetabled around your needs.

On joining the Sixth Form,

a)   you will be placed with a tutor group led by your Personal Tutor who will stay with you throughout your time in Sixth Form.

b)   you will be placed with a tutor group led by your Personal Tutor whom will stay with you throughout your time in Sixth Form.

c)   you will be placed with a tutor group led by your Personal Tutor that will stay with you throughout your time in Sixth Form.

d)   you will be placed with a tutor group led by your Personal Tutor which will stay with you throughout your time in Sixth Form.

During your time at Sixth Form you will develop independent learning skills, so that you are fully equipped for university and working life. You will begin to

a)   take greater responsibility for you're own learning, acquire new study skills and become self-motivated.

b)   take greater responsibility for your own learning, acquiring new study skills and become self-motivated.

c)   take more greater responsibility for your own learning, acquire new study skills and become self-motivated.

d)

take greater responsibility for your own learning, acquire new study skills and become self-motivated.

Reading comprehension (12 marks)

At The Art Council, we believe that great arts and culture should be an integral part of every young person's education. We know that children's engagement in arts and culture drops off after the age of ten, but with the creative industries now generating 1 in 20 new jobs, it is vital that we continue to cultivate young creative talent.

Cultural education sparks creativity across the curriculum, encouraging young people to be inquisitive, disciplined and determined. We believe that every child should have the right to create, compose and perform, as well as visit, experience and participate in extraordinary work. However, we know that not all of them are getting those opportunities. We know that the provision of cultural education is inconsistent. With public finances stretched, and more than eight million pupils in 24,000 schools, we need to develop new ways of working collaboratively to enhance our cultural education infrastructure.

That's why in October this year we launched the Cultural Education Challenge, to encourage sector leaders across the arts, education, local authorities, schools, higher education institutions and others to work together in 'Cultural Education Partnerships' to create joined-up arts and cultural provision across the country.

We want these partnerships to drive clear, visible and coherent local arts and cultural offers, to ensure that more children and young people have access to great arts and culture both inside and outside of school. The partnerships will respond to local needs, whilst maximising local assets, pooling local expertise and developing shared visions and priorities. It will be vital to have the participation and leadership of schools, governors and head teachers in shaping these local partnerships.

The Department for Education supports this. School's Minister, Nick Gibb, spoke at the launch of the Cultural Education Challenge and said; "Not only does cultural education build the cultural literacy of our pupils, it also has the ability to build positive character traits amongst pupils such as confidence, perseverance, and the ability to cooperate with one's peers".

The Governors' handbook now states that 'cultural education forms an important part of a broad and balanced curriculum' and it is a 'legal requirement for both maintained schools and academies to promote the cultural development of their pupils'. Ofsted has also confirmed that school inspections must take account of whether schools offer a broad, balanced and relevant curriculum.

Much has been done already to increase the quality and provision of cultural education for children and young people. Artsmark can help unlock the potential of children and young people, help to develop character and talent, and increase their knowledge and understanding. The new Artsmark award will help schools to deliver a high-quality arts and cultural education and to demonstrate this to Ofsted. Artsmark have access to exceptional resources that will help schools develop and strengthen their arts provision.

Artsmark complements Arts Award, which we run in partnership with Trinity College London, and which recognises the outstanding achievements of individual young people. Music Education Hubs bring together all local music education providers to ensure that every child has the opportunity to engage and progress across musical genres. We have also invested £10 million in ten Bridge organisations across England, which play a crucial role in connecting young people with cultural provisions. Over 7000 schools work with their respective Bridge organisations already.

Working with children and young people is a part of our funding agreements with arts organisations and museums across the country, who will be key partners in designing local cultural education offers. And we are seeing new platforms, partnerships and ways of working. Recent examples include the development of the new TES online platform that gives teachers access to arts and cultural teaching resources from organisations such as the V&A, BFI, and the RSC.

The Arts Council has identified 50 new Cultural Education Partnerships across the country, in areas of most need. They will be modelled on pilot partnerships established in Great Yarmouth, Bristol and Barking & Dagenham, initiated by the Arts Council. Our national Bridge organisations will catalyse and support these partnerships.

We are focused on getting these 50 partnerships up and running by 2018, and we are encouraging other strong convenors to come forward to help deliver the challenge in other areas. It is simply impossible for the partnerships to deliver what pupils and schools need without the input of schools, and we call for all schools, governors and head teachers to get involved in shaping these local partnerships.

Task 1 (2 marks): select 2 most appropriate titles for this article

a)   Ofsted to grade schools on cultural development of pupils

b)   Young people's right to a cultural education

c)   Dance, drama and painting to be driven in schools

d)   Teenagers not interested in arts and culture

e)   Move to boost children's cultural education

f)   Schools not providing cultural opportunities in breach of government reforms

g)   Unlocking children's potential through culture

h)   Cultural Education Partnerships finally on the rise

Task 2 (2 marks): select the most appropriate alternative for each phrase as it appears in the text:

1. "The provision of cultural education is inconsistent" (paragraph 2) is closest in meaning to:

a) cultural education providers are unreliable

b) the cultural education across the country is identical

c) there are variances between the types of cultural education on offer

d) providers of cultural education can provide bespoke programmes

2. "maximising local assets, pooling local expertise" (paragraph 4) is closest in meaning to:

a) using local facilities and local experts to make a profit

b) taking advantage of local facilities and training the locals to become experts

c) making the most of what is available in the area and combining the knowledge of experts in the area

d) using as many local facilities as possible and allowing the experts to use them

Task 3 (4 marks): read the statements below and, based on the evidence provided by the passage, decide whether:

- the statement is **supported** by the text (S)
- the statement is **implied** to be the case or is implicitly supported by the text (I)
- the text provides **no evidence** or information concerning the statement (NE)
- the statement is **implicitly contradicted** or implicitly refuted by the text (IC)
- the statement is **explicitly contradicted** or refuted by the text (EC)

a)   Lack of funding is the main reason why children are missing out on cultural opportunities.

b)   Not every school needs to include cultural education in their curriculum.

c)   Students who have better cultural education opportunities can expect to have better GCSE grades.

d)   It is vital that children receive good cultural education since it will increase their employability in the future.

Task 4 (4 marks): select the four statements that are true:

a) Improvements need to me made regarding cultural education.

b) Local partnerships can improve cultural education without requiring any input from schools.

c) Cultural literacy has other side benefits such as improving children's social skills.

d) Ofsted need to see evidence of cultural education in every lesson observation.

e) The current offer of cultural education is very similar from one educational institution to another.

f) Schools can improve their cultural education offer with the help of local partners.

g) The creation of the Bridge organisations has not been particularly successful.

h) There is currently inadequate funding to guarantee that there is good cultural education provision in all schools.

Literacy test 2 (47 marks)

Spelling (10 marks)

1. The SATS results this year were _____ (unbelievable / unbeleivable / unbeleivible / unbelieveable).

2. There is an online _____ where form tutors can book appointments with the head of year. (calander / calendar / calandar / calender)

3. The pupils must _____ that their behaviour is having a profound effect on teaching and learning. (aknowledge / aknowlidge / acknowledge / acknowlidge)

4. The headteacher is very _____ of the fact that an Ofsted inspection is imminent. (conscious / concious / conscous / conshious)

5. New teachers in this school _____ require a lot of support from the Senior Leadership Team. (definately / definitelly / definitily / definitely)

6. If students contest staff decisions, they are to be removed to the isolation room _____ . (immediately / imediately / immediatelly / immediatley)

7. The school has a strong tradition in modern _____ languages. (foriegn / forign / foreign / foirein)

8. Sue has been made the captain of the girls' football team as she has shown the most _____ . (comitment / committment / comittment / commitment).

9. In the physics lesson, the students needed to use a micrometer screw _____ . (gage / gauge / gaige / gayge)

10. _____ , we can't guarantee that every student will have the opportunity to have their photo taken with the author. (Unfortunately / Unfortunitely / Unfortunatelly / Unfortunitelly),

Punctuation (15 marks)

House System

On entry to Grange hill school every child is placed in a tutor group which is attached to a House there are four Houses in total Coppell, Hodgson, Pulis and Pardew. Students are allocated into Houses at the end of Year 6 taking into account the House identity of any older siblings, in order to promote a sense of tradition within our Grange Hill families. We ensure that each House includes students with a range of talents, abilities and interests to ensure our thriving House system remains competitive. Over 80 sports competitions take place over the school year, and include the following activities netball, hockey football, basketball, volleyball and dodgeball. Students are also able to earn points for their House via whole school events such as the Fundraiser Walk through attendance competitions, and by collecting merits, which is an integral part of our rewards system at Grange Hill School

At Easter, we award the lombardo Trophy to the House earning the most points from sports competitions over the year. At the end of the summer term the Merit Shield is awarded to the House with the most points from students gaining the highest number of Merit Certificates (from the Bronze Certificate to the Headteachers Award.

At the beginning of each year, the students in each House vote for a male and female Sports Captain for each year group. In addition, each form will vote for a Form Representative. The Form Representatives main role is to attend student council meetings throughout the year, and report back to their form on discussions and decisions reached by the School Council.

Grammar (10 marks)

Task 1 (3 marks)

We are delighted that you are considering applying to Grange Hill's Sixth Form. As a Sixth Form we are committed to

a)   insuring that our Christian values remain at the heart of our provision.

b)   ensure that our Christian values remain at the heart of our provision.

c)   insuring that our Christian values remain at the heart of our provision.

d)   ensuring that our Christian values remain at the heart of our provision.

This next step on your educational journey is an extremely important one.

a)   Having worked hard for your GCSE qualifications, you should make sure that the choices you now make are the right ones.

b)   After working hard for your GCSE qualifications, you need to make sure that the choices you now make are the right ones.

c)   Having worked hard for your GCSE qualifications, you need to make sure that the choices you now make are the right ones.

d)   After all the hard work for your GCSE qualifications, you must make sure that the choices you now make are the right ones.

Our curriculum

a)   is broad and balanced, and will allow you to tailor your learning experience to suit your future progression.

b)   is broad and balanced, and allows you to tailor your learning experience to suit your future progression.

c)   is broad and balanced, and allowing you to tailor your learning experience to suit your progression in the future.

d)   is broad and balanced, and will allow you to tailor your learning experience for suitable future progression.

Task 2 (3 marks)

There is no better feeling than

a)   seeing our students achieve the grades and qualifications to move on to university, apprenticeships or the world of work.

b)   seeing our students achieving the grades and qualifications to move on to university, apprenticeships or the world of work.

c)   to see our students achieve the grades and qualifications to move on to university, apprenticeships or the working world.

d)   to see our students achieve the grades and qualifications to move on to university, apprenticeships or the world of work.

For this to happen,

a)   there might be a combination of academic rigour, high quality pastoral care and outstanding teaching and learning.

b)   there can be a combination of academic rigour, high quality pastoral care and outstanding teaching and learning.

c)   there should be a combination of academic rigour, high quality pastoral care and outstanding teaching and learning.

d)   there must be a combination of academic rigour, high quality pastoral care and outstanding teaching and learning.

Grange Hill has

a)   an exceptional reputation for it's values, care and achievement and, as a member of our Sixth Form, you will receive outstanding support.

b)   an exceptional reputation for its values, care and achievement and, as a member of our Sixth Form, you will receive outstanding support.

c)   an exceptional reputation for its' values, care and achievement and, as a member of our Sixth Form, you receive outstanding support.

d)   an exceptional reputation for its values, care and achievement and, as a member of our Sixth Form, you receive outstanding support.

Task 3 (4 marks)

Huddersfield Special Educational Needs Support Service

a)   provides information, advise and support to parents, carers, children and young people

b)   provides information, advise and support to parent's, carer's, children and young people

c)   provides information, advice and support to parents, carers, children and young people

d)   provides information, advice and support to parents', carers', children and young people

in relation to Special Educational Needs and related health and social care issues.

Our service is free and

a)   can be provided over the telephone, during home visits or through support at meetings concerning SEN and disability.

b)   may be provided over the telephone, during home visits or through support at meetings concerning SEN and disability.

c)   should be provided over the telephone, during home visits or through support at meetings concerning SEN and disability.

d)   is going to be provided over the telephone, during home visits or through support at meetings concerning SEN and disability.

a)   Many children can access information and support via there parents,

b)   Many children will access information and support via their parents,

c)   Many children will access information and support via they're parents,

d)   Many children should access information and support via they're parents,

but older children and young people may want to access the service themselves. The service can:

a)   help you understand educational support in schools, giving support in relation to a My Support Plan, which may include future reviews, explain the law and your rights, helping when things go wrong.

b)   help you understand educational support in schools, give support in relation to a My Support Plan, which may include attending meetings, explain the law and your rights, and helping when things go wrong

c)   help you understand educational support in schools, give support in relation to a My Support Plan, which may include future reviews, explaining the law and your rights, and help when things go wrong.

d)   help you understand educational support in schools, give support in relation to a My Support Plan, which may include future reviews, explain the law and your rights, and help when things go wrong.

Reading comprehension (12 marks)

Why is it that some schools continue to struggle with managing and improving behaviour?

At a recent event at King Solomon Academy in Paddington, I gathered together a group of headteachers of outstanding schools who succeed with some of the most deprived pupils in England. I asked them to outline what they felt were the key principles that they had followed for improving behaviour in their schools. What soon became clear was how much similarity there was between the approaches that the headteachers had followed. Many of them emphasised the simplicity of their approach, but they agreed that most important of all is consistency.

Where there is inconsistency in schools, children are more likely to push the boundaries. If a pupil thinks there is a chance that the school will forget about the detention he has been given, then he is unlikely to bother to turn up. If he gets away with it, the threat of detention will be no deterrent in the future.

Often it is doing the simple things that can make a difference with behaviour. For example, the teacher who takes the time to meet and greet pupils at the door will find they come in happier and ready to learn.

I recently read the 'Checklist Manifesto' by Atul Gawande, a surgeon who was concerned that so many patients seemed to suffer serious complications in the days after their operation. He realised that many of these problems were caused by operating staff failing to follow basic procedures. For example, a surgeon failing to wash his hands could cause an infection, or failing to account for all the swabs used in the process could lead to one being left in the patient's body.

Gawande developed a checklist to be read out before each operation to ensure that all of the simple, but essential procedures were followed. The outcome was a marked decrease in the number of patients becoming seriously ill or dying after surgery.

I took the idea of a checklist and adapted it to help schools to improve behaviour. My list is a menu of ideas from which schools can develop their own checklist. The list is not exhaustive and some parts would apply just to secondary or to primary schools. School staff or headteachers decide what their priorities are for improving behaviour and then create a bespoke checklist of between five and 10 essential actions to promote good behaviour. The teachers run through the checklist first thing in the morning and again after lunch to ensure the correct preparations are in place. It serves as a reminder of what needs to be done and ensures consistency across the school.

I have asked some schools to look at areas of behaviour they want to improve and devise their own checklist. Examples have included:

1. making sure all adults in the room know how to respond to sensitive pupils with special needs;
2. ensuring that children actually receive rewards every time they have earned them and receive a sanction every time they behave badly;
3. having a list of classroom non-negotiables which the students know you will always sanction;
4. carefully following each stage of the behaviour policy rather than overreacting to poor behaviour;
5. simply remembering to stay calm.

Teachers who follow these guidelines find there is more consistency of approach to managing behaviour, both in the classroom and around the school. When children know that teachers will stick to the behaviour policy and class routines, they feel safer and happy, and behaviour improves.

The checklist may seem too simple, but managing a school or a class is a complex operation and because of this complexity it is easy to fail to get the simple, but essential, things right. After all, who could have believed patients die in hospitals because staff fail to wash their hands properly?

In the special school where I am headteacher, we have considerable expertise with the most challenging behaviour. Yet a few years ago, one of my teaching assistants pointed out that we had become very good at ensuring children got the sanctions they had earned, but they were not getting their rewards with the same consistency. The message we were inadvertently sending to our pupils was that your good behaviour is less important to us than the things you are doing wrong. A checklist would have stopped us getting into this situation.

Like Gawande's checklists for surgeons, mine are not written in tablets of stone and purporting to be perfect. They have been tested in a few schools who have gone on to develop and refine them to suit their own particular context , just as surgeons are now doing in hospitals. This is the start of a grassroots project led by heads and teachers – not a Government initiative in which schools are told what to do.

Task 1 (2 marks): select the two most appropriate titles for this article:

a)   Don't let poor behaviour get in the way

b)   Simple checklists for behaviour management

c)   Schools facing tough new behavioural guidelines

d)   Teachers to copy surgeons to combat classroom behaviour

e)   Getting the simple things right

f)   Teachers struggling to manage students in the classroom

g)   Ofsted to clamp down on teachers who can't control their students

h)   Schools are inconsistent with behaviour management

Task 2 (4 marks): select the four statements that are true:

a) School behaviour policies should have as many basic rules as possible, so that the students are in no doubt about what they should and shouldn't be doing at all times.

b) It is important than children learn that their good behaviour is just as important in a school as avoiding negative behaviour.

c) Children are happier in a classroom environment where the rules are vague as they are more able to misbehave without receiving sanctions.

d) Managing children is hard which is why behaviour policies need to be simple.

e) Schools should all have the same priorities on their lists for managing behaviour.

f) Threats have to be followed through for them to have any meaning.

g) The key principles for improving behaviour in schools is consistency and simplicity.

h) If you only focus on positive behaviour, eventually students will meet expectations without the need for threats and sanctions.

Task 3 (4 marks): by comparing to the original list which appears in the passage, select the four most appropriate statements to complete the missing parts of this bulleted list.

I have asked some schools to look at areas of behaviour they want to improve and devise their own checklist. Examples have included:

1.
2.
3.
4.
5.   simply remembering to stay calm.

a)   focusing on the positives in the classroom rather than dwelling on the negatives;

b)   remembering that it is the behaviour you are tackling and not the individual, so your response to every child must be exactly the same;

c)   ensuring that staff have had the correct training and use the correct procedures with the more vulnerable students;

d)   remembering to record house points on the school system, or to write positive comments in student planners when you have promised this, and not forgetting to carry out what you have threatened when students are failing to meet expectations;

e)   having a few basic rules in your classroom which the students are aware of and which you sanction without hesitation;

f)   in the first few lessons of the academic year only, ensuring your classroom presence is intimidating so that the students quickly understand you are in control;

g)   not allowing emotion to overcome you, and simply following what your school expects you to do step by step;

h)   remembering that, even though every lesson is a fresh start for a student, if students continue to fail to respond to your expectations, they can be fast-tracked through the steps of the classroom behaviour policy;

Task 4 (2 marks): the following groups might all be potential audiences or readers of the article, although some of them would find it more useful than others. Which group would find it the most relevant and which group would find it the least relevant?

a)   headteachers

b)   pastoral support staff

c)   Ofsted inspectors

d)   parents

e)   classroom teachers in general

f)   heads of year / house

g)   government ministers

h)   students

Literacy test 3 (47 marks)

Spelling (10 marks)

1. Haley's Comet is an _____ that takes place approximately every seventy-six years. (occurence / occurrance / occurance / occurrence)

2. This class is a joy to teach as there are so many _____ learners. (independant / independent / indipendent / indipendant)

3. The student _____ meet on alternate Fridays in the common room. (comittee / commitee / committee / comitee)

4. The students are not showing enough _____ with the 5 mark questions. (perserverance / perseverence / perserveerence / perseverance)

5. The _____ is closed on Friday afternoons. (library / libracy / libarry / libary)

6. Written sources are considered virtually _____ for today's history teaching. (indispensible / indispensabel / indespensable / indispensable)

7. Due to temporary _____, the gym will not be open at lunchtime this week. (maintainance / maintainence / maintenance / maintenance)

8. It is hard to _____ the diverse needs of every child in this group. (acomodate / accomadate / accommodate / accommadate)

9. Key words need to be written on the whiteboard, especially the words which the students commonly _____ . (misspell / mispell / mispel / misspel)

10. In the experiment, the class were asked to _____ the crystal from the solution. (seperate / sepparate / separate / sepperate)

Punctuation (15 marks)

Exam timetable

This year the GCSE exam period runs from May 13 to June 18. Please remember that you need to remain available to sit exams until June 26, as the exam boards have nominated this as a 'contingency day in the event of a national disruption to exams; your parents / carers were informed of this in the autumn term. You have been given a copy of your exam timetable, but if you need another copy please see ms Smith or call in at the main office.

You should arrive in school before 8.50 for exams timetabled for 9.00 and before 1.00pm for exams timetabled for 1.30. Unfortunately, Exam Boards may not accept your paper if you arrive late if you think you are going to be late for an exam, you (or your parent / carer must call school immediately so we can tell you what you need to do in your particular situation.

Exam regulations

The school has to implement a very precise set of rules in all public exams, and we are inspected during each GCSE exam period to ensure we are meeting the standards expected a copy of these regulations for both written and onscreen tests is attached. The latter is only relevant to students taking GCSE computer science. Please read this information carefully, to ensure you do not inadvertently break the rules and risk disqualification. Please note that no potential technological or webenabled source of information including mobile phones, ipods, smart watches), may be taken into the exam room. Possession of such a device could result in disqualification even if its switched off and you do not intend to use it.

Grammar (10 marks)

Task 1 (4 marks)

Dear Sixth Form,

On the first day of term

a)   I would of mentioned that some of you will have a good idea as to what life holds in 6 form,

b)   I would have mentioned that some of you will have a good idea as to what life holds in store,

c)   I could have mentioned that some of you will have a good idea as to what life holds in store,

d)   I could of mentioned that some of you will have a good idea as to what life holds in store,

but wherever we may be in life, there are certain core principles:

When faced with two choices, choose the harder option. The things we do for others

a)   is more rewarding than those that we do for ourselves.

b)   is more rewarding than those what we do for ourselves.

c)   are more rewarding than those that we do for ourselves.

d)   are more rewarding than those that we do for us.

Time shall pass,

a) so enjoy the good times, and don't worry about the bad times as they should go by.

b) so enjoy the good times, and don't worry about the bad times as they can go by.

c) so enjoy the good times, and don't worry about the bad times as they could go by.

d) so enjoy the good times, and don't worry about the bad times as they will go by.

In your future life, remember the need to balance the 'three legs of the stool':

a) whatever job you may do must satisfy three needs: material, intellectual and spiritual.

b) whatever job you can do ought to satisfy three needs: material, intellectual and spiritual.

c) whatever job you will needs to satisfy three needs: material, intellectual and spiritual.

d) whatever job you do must satisfy three needs: material, intellectual and spiritual.

Task 2 (3 marks)

Dear Parent or Carer,

We are carrying out research and information gathering around the possibility of introducing a Chromebook purchase scheme.

We have been talking to schools

a)   who have already introduced this type of scheme

b)   who have already introduced these type of schemes

c)   who have already introduced these types of scheme

d)   who have already introduced this types of schemes

about how it has had a positive impact on their teaching and learning and what the benefits this type of approach bring to the school.

Please click on the below link to read a case study of

a)   how the scheme had helped develop engagement and learning outcomes.

b)   how the scheme will have helped develop engagement and learning outcomes.

c)   how the scheme has helped develop engagement and learning outcomes.

d)   how the scheme should have helped develop engagement and learning outcomes.

We therefore would like to know if

a) this is something you could consider and are inviting you to complete the below survey.

b) this is something you should consider and would invite you to complete the below survey.

c) this is something you could consider and invite you to complete the below survey.

d) this is something you would consider and invite you to complete the below survey.

Task 3 (3 marks)

In the unlikely event of the school

a) needs to close at short notice during the school day, the following arrangements will come into effect:

b) having to close at short notice during the school day, the following arrangements will come into effect:

c) has to close at short notice during the school day, the arrangements that follow will come into effect:

d) having to close at short notice during the school day, the arrangements that follow will come into effect:

a) Closure may be linked to the bus companie's decisions;

b) Closure may be linked to the bus companies decision's;

c) Closure may be linked to the bus companies' decisions;

d) Closure may be linked to the bus company decisions;

they sometimes cancel, or bring forward, services in poor weather conditions.

Whatever the cause, if the decision to close is made,

a) students will be assembling in their tutor room and the Leadership Group will communicate protocols with staff.

b) students will assemble in their tutor room and the Leadership Group will communicate protocols with staff.

c) students would assemble in their tutor room and the Leadership Group should communicate protocols with staff.

d) students will assemble in their tutor room and the Leadership Group can communicate protocols with staff.

Reading comprehension (12 marks)

Effective marking is an essential part of the education process. At its heart, it is an interaction between teacher and pupil: a way of acknowledging pupils' work, checking the outcomes and making decisions about what teachers and pupils need to do next, with the primary aim of driving pupil progress. This can often be achieved without extensive written dialogue or comments.

Our starting point is that marking – providing written feedback on pupils' work – has become disproportionately valued by schools and has become unnecessarily burdensome for teachers. There are a number of reasons for this, including the impact of Government policy, what has been promoted by Ofsted, and decisions taken by school leaders and teachers. This is not to say that all marking should be eliminated, but that it must be proportionate.

The quantity of feedback should not be confused with the quality. The quality of the feedback, however given, will be seen in how a pupil is able to tackle subsequent work.

Marking is a vital element of teaching, but when it is ineffective it can be demoralising and a waste of time for teachers and pupils alike. In particular, we are concerned that it has become common practice for teachers to provide extensive written comments on every piece of work when there is very little evidence that this improves pupil outcomes in the long term.

There is also a cultural challenge here. In many cases the view is that you must spend hours marking to be a good teacher; that writing pages of feedback makes you more effective; and that there is a link between the quantity of marking and pupil progress. These are myths that need to be debunked.

There is no 'one-size-fits-all' approach. A balance needs to be struck between a core and consistent approach and trusting teachers to focus on what is best for their pupils and circumstances.

In summary, we recommend that all marking should be meaningful, manageable and motivating. This should be the perspective adopted by all engaged in education, from classroom teachers to the Department for Education (DfE).

Marking has evolved into an unhelpful burden for teachers, when the time it takes is not repaid in positive impact on pupils' progress. This is frequently because it is serving a different purpose such as demonstrating teacher performance or to satisfy the requirements of other, mainly adult, audiences. Too often, it is the marking itself which is being monitored and commented on by leaders rather than pupil outcomes and progress as a result of quality feedback.

The consequence of this skewed dominance of written feedback means that teachers have less time to focus on the most important aspect of their job – teaching pupils. There are also wider implications for the workforce: cutting out the unnecessary frequency and depth of marking to create a manageable workload has clear benefits in retaining experienced teachers and supporting newly qualified teachers as they concentrate on what attracted them to the profession in the first place: making a difference to pupils.

Our remit was to pay particular attention to 'deep marking'. From a review of the educational literature, there appears to be no broadly agreed definition for this term or any theoretical underpinning of its educational worth. As a working definition we adopted the following: 'Deep marking is a generic term used to describe a process whereby teachers provide written feedback to pupils offering guidance with a view to improving or enhancing the future performance of pupils. Pupils are then expected to respond in writing to the guidance which in turn is verified by the teacher.'

Deep marking also seems to have been supported by an assumption that marking provides a more thorough means of giving feedback and demonstrates a stronger professional ethic, as well as improving pupil outcomes. Deep marking often acts as a proxy for 'good' teaching as it is something concrete and tangible which lends itself as 'evidence'. In some cases, the perception exists that the amount of marking a teacher does equals their level of professionalism and effectiveness. These are false assumptions.

We considered what ineffective marking looks like:

· It usually involves an excessive reliance on the labour-intensive practices under our definition of deep marking, such as extensive written comments in different colour pens

· It can be disjointed from the learning process, failing to help pupils improve their understanding. This can be because work is set and marked to a false timetable, and based on a policy of following a mechanistic timetable, rather than responding to pupils' needs.

· It can be dispiriting, for both teacher and pupil, by failing to encourage and engender motivation and resilience.

· It can be unmanageable for teachers, and teachers forced to mark work late at night and at weekends are unlikely to operate effectively in the classroom.

Task 1 (2 marks): select the two most appropriate titles for this article:

a)   Ineffective marking making teachers' lives a misery

b)   Teachers marking to protect themselves rather than to help the children

c)   Deep marking in schools set to end, to the relief of teachers

d)   Eliminating unnecessary workload around marking

e)   Students making inadequate progress due to lack of marking

f)   Schools urged to review marking policies to halt teacher decline

g)   Schools marking policies must be effective and efficient

h)   Teachers' marking wasted on most students

Task 2 (4 marks): select the four statements that are true:

a)   The amount of feedback teachers give is of great importance.

b)   Teachers would perform better in the classroom if more efficient marking policies were in place.

c)   A school needs to agree on a marking policy which all teaching staff must adhere to for the sake of consistency.

d)   For marking to be effective, you must only write in one colour.

e)   Senior leaders should be focusing on student outcomes rather than the quality of marking.

f)   The amount of deep marking carried out by a teacher speaks volumes for their effectiveness as a teacher.

g)   There is no proof that deep marking has any impact on student progress.

h)   Some schools place too much importance on the need for written feedback in students' books.

Task 3 (4 marks): read the statements below and, based on the evidence provided by the passage, decide whether:

- the statement is **supported** by the text (S)
- the statement is **implied** to be the case or is implicitly supported by the text (I)
- the text provides **no evidence** or information concerning the statement (NE)
- the statement is **implicitly contradicted** or implicitly refuted by the text (IC)
- the statement is **explicitly contradicted** or refuted by the text (EC)

a)   There are teachers who cover up for their weaknesses by ensuring that their marking is regular and detailed.

b)   Teachers are sometimes having to mark books when dictated by policy rather than the teacher's own professional judgement.

c)   There is a direct link between the length of written comments from teachers and long-term pupil progress.

d)   Deep marking is a complete waste of a teacher's and a pupil's time.

Task 4 (2 marks): select the most appropriate alternative for each phrase as it appears in the text:

1. "has become disproportionately valued by schools and has become unnecessarily burdensome for teachers" (paragraph 2) is closest in meaning to:

a) schools believe there is no value, so teachers don't believe the work is necessary

b) schools don't believe it to be valuable, but teachers do it anyway, even though it is not necessary

c) schools believe it to be extremely valuable, but it creates too much work for teachers

d) the amount of time teachers spend doing it means schools should value it more

2. "there appears to be .... no theoretical underpinning of its educational worth" (paragraph 10) is closest in meaning to:

a) there may be no theory behind it, but it is important nonetheless

b) according to theories, it is very worthwhile in an educational setting

c) in the absence of any theory to back it up, it has been proven to be reliable

d) in the absence of theory to prove otherwise, it has not been proven to benefit education at all

Literacy test 4 (47 marks)

Spelling (10 marks)

1. _____ students may be placed on report for having a poor attitude to learning. (Occasionally / Ocasionally / Occassionally / Occasionaly)

2. All teaching _____ were asked to evacuate the building. (personal / personale / personnel / personelle)

3. All expenses will be reimbursed on return provided that all _____ are handed in. (receits / reciepts / receets / receipts)

4. Since the weather is very _____ , we will make a decision on Friday regarding the Duke of Edinburgh expedition. (changable / changeable / changeible / changible)

5. The students has been _____ to CAMS for an assessment. (referred / refferred / reffered / refered)

6. Teachers may provide _____ for students, provided they have known them for at least three years. (referances / references / refferences / referrances)

7. Belinda spends a lot of time in the isolation room as she is a very _____ (mischievous / mischievious / mischeivous / mischeivious) pupil.

8. The teacher's _____ of French is good, but he has a noticeably English accent. (pronunciation / pronounciation / pronownciation / pronunciacion)

9. Some of the students do not think that the lesson is _____ to them. (relivant / relevent / relivent / relevant)

10. The student moved in _____ with the music. (rhthym / rhythm / rythm / ritham)

Punctuation (15 marks)

Performance Sports Programme

Specialist highlevel coaching, as part of a Performance Sports Programme is provided for those students wishing to pursue their chosen sport and represent that sport at county level or above.

Sports options in the programme include athletics, basketball, cricket, football, rugby, netball hockey and swimming

Each students programme follows a unique scheme of work, including the latest tactical, technical, physical and mental training they are designed with a focus on individual talent development, and present opportunities for students to develop their skills right through to uK and international competition. The Sports Science Centre provides students with a movement-analysis testing and monitoring facility, together with equipment designed for assessing a broad range of health and fitness indicators. The Sports Treatment Centre has world class equipment ranging from underwater treadmills to cryotherapy cold spa baths, to help students rehabilitation and posttraining recovery.

Importantly all Performance Sport students are enrolled within the Faculty, where the flexibility of the curriculum allows them to combine their sporting programme with a range of options in GCSE A-level and BTEC courses in both Key Stages 4 and 5. This enables them to maintain a wellrounded education whilst pursuing their passion. They also have access to a strong network of pastoral and academic support, including Tutors, Heads of Year, and Academic Learning Mentors.

Grammar (10 marks)

Task 1 (4 marks)

All forms of bullying (including cyberbullying) should be handled as a community issue for the whole school.

It is important

a) that schools must take measures to prevent and tackle bullying among pupils.

b) that schools should take measures to prevent and tackle bullying among pupils.

c) that schools take measures to prevent and tackle bullying among pupils.

d) that schools take measures to prevent and tackle bullying within pupils.

Evidence indicates that one in five teachers

a) have reported having derogatory comments posted about them on social media sites.

b) had reported having derogatory comments posted about them on social media sites.

c) had reported having had derogatory comments posted about them on social media sites.

d) have reported to have had derogatory comments posted about them on social media sites.

School leaders, teachers, school staff, parents and pupils all have rights and responsibilities in relation to cyberbullying

a)   and should work together to create an environment free from bullying in which pupils can learn, and staff can have fulfilling careers.

b)   and need to work together to create an environment free from bullying in which pupils need to learn, and staff will have fulfilling careers.

c)   and can work together to create an environment free from bullying in which pupils can learn, and staff can have fulfilling careers.

d)   and will work together to create an environment free from bullying in which pupils will learn, and staff will have fulfilling careers.

Schools can offer support to parents on

a)   how to help their children safely and responsibly engage with social media, perhaps through a parents' evening, or advice in a school newsletter.

b)   how to help their children engage safely and responsibly with social media, perhaps through a parents' evening, or advice in a school newsletter.

c)   how to help their children engage safely and responsibly with social media, perhaps through a parents' evening, or advise in a school newsletter.

d)   how to help their children safely and responsibly engage with social media, perhaps through a parents' evening, or advise in a school newsletter.

Task 2 (3 marks)

Preparing your coursework – good practice

a)   If you receive help and guidance by someone who is not your teacher,

b)   If you receive help and guidance through someone other than your teacher,

c)   If you receive help and guidance from someone other than your teacher,

d)   If you receive help and guidance from someone who is not your teacher,

you must tell your teacher, who will then record

a)   the nature of the assistance he has given to you.

b)   the type of assistance he had given to you.

c)   the type of assistance given to you.

d)   the nature of the assistance given to you.

Your parent/carer may provide you with access to resource materials and discuss your coursework with

you.

a)   Moreover, they must not give you direct advice on what should and should not be included.

b)   Furthermore, they must not give you direct advice on what should and should not be included.

c)   However, they must not give you direct advice on what should and should not be included.

d)   Additionally, they must not give you direct advice on what should and should not be included.

Task 3 (3 marks)

Sixth Form Curriculum Information

I am pleased to write with further details of our resources and events

a)   to help support students in making there choices regarding post-16 study.

b)   to help supporting students in making their choices about post-16 study.

c)   to help support students in making their choices regarding post-16 study.

d)   to help support students to make there choices regarding post-16 study.

Firstly, please find here an electronic copy of our Post-16 Curriculum Information booklet

a)   that we are hoping will prove useful in answering any questions you may have about A level studies.

b)   that we hope will prove useful in answering any questions you will have about A level studies.

c)   that we hope will prove useful in answering any questions you may have about A level studies.

d)   that we will hope proves useful in answering any questions you have about A level studies.

The booklet gives information about the wide range of opportunities available to our sixth form,

a)   both in the subjects they can choose and the wider activities that we encourage our student to participate in.

b)   both in the subjects they may choose and the wider activities that we encourage our students to participate in.

c)   both in the subjects they choose and the wider activities that we are encouraging our student to participate in.

d)   both in the subjects they are choosing and the wider activities that we can encourage our students to participate in.

Reading comprehension (12 marks)

The headteacher of the institution in which an NQT is serving an induction period is responsible for ensuring that the supervision and training of the NQT meets their development needs. The duties assigned to the NQT and the conditions under which they work should be such as to facilitate a fair and effective assessment of the NQT's conduct and efficiency as a teacher against the relevant standards.

In particular, a suitable post must:

1. have a headteacher to make the recommendation about whether the NQT's performance against the relevant standards is satisfactory;
2. have prior agreement with an appropriate body to act in this role to quality assure the induction process;
3. provide the NQT with the necessary employment tasks, experience and support to enable them to demonstrate satisfactory performance against the 12 relevant standards throughout and by the end of the induction period;
4. ensure the appointment of an induction tutor with QTS;
5. provide the NQT with a reduced timetable to enable them to undertake activities in their induction programme;
6. not make unreasonable demands upon the NQT;
7. not normally demand teaching outside the age range and/or subject(s) for which the NQT has been employed to teach;
8. not present the NQT, on a day-to-day basis, with discipline problems that are unreasonably demanding for the setting;
9. involve the NQT regularly teaching the same class(es);
10. involve similar planning, teaching and assessment processes to those in which other teachers working in similar substantive posts in the institution are engaged;
11. not involve additional non-teaching responsibilities without the provision of appropriate preparation and support

Section A

In a relevant school, the headteacher must ensure an NQT has a reduced timetable of no more than 90% of the timetable of the school's existing teachers on the main pay range to enable them to undertake activities in their induction programme.

Section B

The length of the induction period an NQT is required to serve, whether the teaching post in which they are doing so is part-time or full-time, is the full-time equivalent of one school year (usually three school terms).

Section C

The minimum period of employment that can be counted towards completion of the induction period (for both full-time and part-time NQTs) is one term (based on an institution that operates three terms in an academic year). This applies to both permanent and long-term supply teaching posts. It also reflects the need for each NQT to work in a stable environment and receive a personalised, supported and pre-planned induction programme. In addition, it is important that the NQT is in post long enough to enable a fair and reasonable assessment to be made of their performance.

NQTs serving induction on a part-time basis at any point will need to serve the full-time equivalent (FTE) of one full academic year. Therefore an NQT working part-time as a 0.5 FTE will need to serve induction for two academic years.

Section D

A suitable monitoring and support programme must be put in place for the NQT, personalised to meet their professional development needs (including the development needs of part-time NQTs). This must include:

1. Support and guidance from a designated induction tutor who holds QTS and has the time and experience to carry out the role effectively
2. Observation of the NQT's teaching and follow-up discussion
3. Regular professional reviews of progress
4. NQT's observation of experienced teachers either in the NQT's own institution or in another institution where effective practice has been identified

Section E

The headteacher must identify a person to act as the NQT's induction tutor, to provide day-to-day monitoring and support, and coordination of assessment. The induction tutor must hold QTS and have the necessary skills and knowledge to work successfully in this role and should be able to provide effective coaching and mentoring. This is a very important element of the induction process and the induction tutor must be given sufficient time to carry out the role effectively and to meet the needs of the NQT. The induction tutor will need to be able to make rigorous and fair judgements about the NQT's progress in relation to the relevant standards. They will need to be able to recognise when early action is needed in the case of an NQT who is experiencing difficulties. It may, in some circumstances, be appropriate for the headteacher to be the induction tutor.

Section F

An NQT's teaching should be observed at regular intervals throughout their induction period to facilitate a fair and effective assessment of the NQT's teaching practice, conduct and efficiency against the relevant standards. Observations of the NQT may be undertaken by the induction tutor or another suitable person who holds QTS from inside or outside the institution.

The NQT and the observer should meet to review any teaching that has been observed. Feedback should be prompt and constructive. Arrangements for review meetings should be made in advance and a brief written record made on each occasion. It should indicate where any development needs have been identified. Professional progress reviews of the NQT

The induction tutor should review the NQT's progress at frequent intervals throughout the induction period. Reviews should be informed by evidence of the NQT's teaching. Objectives should be reviewed and revised in relation to the relevant standards and the needs and strengths of the individual NQT. The NQT should record evidence of progress towards objectives and agreed steps to support them in meeting their objectives. Evidence should come from practice.

Section G

NQTs should have formal assessments carried out by either the headteacher or the induction tutor. These could be undertaken on a termly basis so that they have three per year. It is for institutions and NQTs to agree exactly when the assessment dates are set, which should occur as near to the end of each term as possible. Evidence used in assessments must be clear and transparent and copies provided to the NQT and appropriate body.

Formal assessment meetings should be informed by evidence gathered during the preceding assessment period and drawn from the NQT's work as a teacher and from their induction programme. Judgements made during the induction period should relate directly to the relevant standards. NQTs should be kept up to date on 18 their progress. There should be no surprises.

The final assessment meeting is at the end of the induction period, and will form the basis of the headteacher's recommendation to the appropriate body as to whether, having completed their induction period, the NQT's performance against the relevant standards is satisfactory, unsatisfactory, or whether or not an extension should be considered. This recommendation should be recorded on the final assessment form.

Task 1 (4 marks): select the four statements that are true:

a) The headteacher should never be the induction tutor.

b) NQTs are expected to work in conditions which gives them the opportunity to demonstrate their abilities as a teacher.

c) It is not a requirement for the induction tutor to hold Qualified Teaching Status.

d) Any experience which is less than a school term is invalid for the purposes of counting towards the induction period of one academic year.

e) NQT lesson observation are only to be carried out by the induction tutor or the headteacher.

f) All NQTs will have their formal assessments on the same day.

g) NQTs are expected to continue observing other teachers to see good practice.

h) It is not a requirement for the NQT to always be observed by the induction tutor.

Task 2 (2 marks): select the appropriate headings for section A and section E

a)   Ensuring a reduced timetable

b)   Determining the length of the induction period

c)   Minimum period of continuous employment that can count towards induction

d)   Appointment of an induction tutor

e)   Observation of the NQT's teaching practice

f)   Monitoring, support and assessment during induction

g)   Formal assessments

Task 3 (4 marks): by comparing to the original list which appears in the passage, select the four most appropriate statements to complete the missing parts of this bulleted list.

In particular, a suitable post must:

1. have a headteacher to make the recommendation about whether the NQT's performance against the relevant standards is satisfactory;
2. have prior agreement with an appropriate body to act in this role to quality assure the induction process;
3. provide the NQT with the necessary employment tasks, experience and support to enable them to demonstrate satisfactory performance against the 12 relevant standards throughout and by the end of the induction period;
4.
5.
6. not make unreasonable demands upon the NQT;
7. not normally demand teaching outside the age range and/or subject(s) for which the NQT has been employed to teach;
8. not present the NQT, on a day-to-day basis, with discipline problems that are unreasonably demanding for the setting;
9. involve the NQT regularly teaching the same class(es);
10.
11.

a) ensure that the expectations for all NQTs within the same educational establishment are the same

b) ensure that the NQT achieves all the teaching standards

c) ensure that the NQT gains some experience of pastoral issues

d) ensure that the NQT is not following a timetable for regular classroom teachers

e) provide access to a tutor with the required qualifications

f)   ensure that the NQT is provided with as many difficult classes as possible in order to gain behaviour management experience

g)   ensure that the NQT is not assigned duties beyond the classroom

h)   ensure that there are weekly training and development sessions for all NQTs in order to develop and embed good practice

Task 4 (2 marks): the following groups might all be potential audiences or readers of the article, although some of them would find it more useful than others. Which group would find it the most relevant and which group would find it the least relevant?

a)   headteachers

b)   newly qualified teachers (NQTs)

c)   Ofsted inspectors

d)   parents

e)   classroom teachers in general

f)   government ministers

g)   PGCE students

h)   university PGCE tutors

Answers

	Numeracy test 1		Numeracy test 2
1.	38.64	1.	4 hours 30 minutes
2.	£50.40	2.	850
3.	4.5	3.	1 hour and 30 minutes
4.	£26,260	4.	75 children
5.	£20	5.	10.6 seconds
6.	14:10	6.	£660
7.	1000 coins	7.	11 months
8.	14	8.	14:40
9.	4 years and 7 months	9.	£14.25
10.	12 metres	10.	13
11.	500g	11.	4
12.	£30	12.	22
13.	£247.50	13.	6:14
14.	61.8	14.	AUS $447
15.	4/7	15.	26p
16.	51%	16.	9.7%
17.	Pupil A	17.	61.5
18.	7	18.	192
19.	C	19.	B
20.	12 years and 6 months	20.	12 years 5 months
21.	A and B	21.	A, B and C
22.	B and C	22.	A and B
23.	12	23.	4
24.	6	24.	45
25.	23%	25.	A and B
26.	A and B	26.	71%
27.	46	27.	23
28.	33%	28.	576 metres squared

	Numeracy test 3		Numeracy test 4
1.	1060	1.	88
2.	48%	2.	22
3.	£36	3.	85%
4.	£3.32	4.	25
5.	45 miles	5.	320
6.	16	6.	£33.50
7.	£46.20	7.	AUS $45
8.	30	8.	150
9.	£11.25	9.	£33,280
10.	1835	10.	1/3
11.	64	11.	£100
12.	90	12.	1530
13.	1345	13.	£26
14.	£80	14.	3
15.	A and B	15.	51%
16.	2	16.	£2.80
17.	100	17.	11
18.	D	18.	A
19.	B and C	19.	

	Numeracy test 3		Numeracy test 4
20.	32%	20.	C
21.	B and C	21.	A and C
22.	A, B and C	22.	B and C
23.	A and B	23.	2/3
24.	1/5	24.	30
25.	65	25.	A and C
26.	A	26.	Grange Hill
27.	33%	27.	60%
28.	9	28.	6

Literacy test 1

Spelling

1. Differentiation
2. Liaison
3. Unnecessary
4. Acceptable
5. Discipline
6. Stationery
7. Embarrassment
8. Accidentally
9. Millennium
10. apparent

Punctuation

Dear Parent / Carer, **(insert comma)**

Please find enclosed a copy of your child's **(insert apostrophe)** mock examination results. Students will have received these results in their lessons, but we thought it would be useful and informative for you to receive a copy of all your child's results on one page.

The **(new paragraph)** mock examination results exist to give students practice of revision and of sitting formal examinations. **(insert full stop)** They **(capital letter)** are very useful for identifying gaps in knowledge, **(insert comma)** skills to improve, or aspects of examination technique to refine. In order to help you interpret your child's result, **(insert comma)** teachers have been asked to signify whether an examination grade is a 'cause **(insert opening inverted commas)** for concern'. This indicates that a change of approach is needed, and that your child will have to speak immediately with their teacher, and act on the advice they are given in order to improve their grade.

It is possible that your child scored a much lower grade than they are currently being tracked at (and **(open brackets)** hope to achieve) in the real examinations, but this has not been identified as a problem. **(insert full stop)** This **(capital latter)** does not mean that the teacher has lowered his or her expectations for your child, but that the reason for the underperformance is easily fixable.

In your discussions with your child about their mock results, **(insert comma)** please emphasise the key message that the mocks represent the beginning of the revision process and that there is plenty of time before the GCSE take place in May **(capital latter)**. Your child should look beyond their overall grade in a subject, regardless of whether it is better or worse than expected, and focus on what they need to do to improve next time.

Where you have any queries about an individual subject, please contact the appropriate teacher. **(insert full stop)** If **(capital letter)** you are concerned more broadly about the performance of your child, please contact the Head of Year.

Grammar

Task 1 – BAB

Task 2 – BAD

Task 3 – CBAD

Reading Comprehension

Task 1 – B, E

Task 2 – 1C, 2C

Task 3 – A – supported, B – explictly contradicted, C – no evidence, D – implied

Task 4 – ACFH

Literacy test 2

Spelling

1. unbelievable
2. calendar
3. acknowledge
4. conscious

5. definitely
6. immediately
7. foreign
8. commitment
9. gauge
10. unfortunately

Punctuation

House System

On entry to Grange Hill **(capital letter)** school, **(insert comma)** every child is placed in a tutor group which is attached to a House. **(insert full stop)** There **(capital letter)** are four Houses in total: **(insert colon)** Coppell, Hodgson, Pulis and Pardew. Students are allocated into Houses at the end of Year 6, **(insert comma)** taking into account the House identity of any older siblings in order to promote a sense of tradition within our Grange Hill families. We ensure that each House includes students with a range of talents, abilities and interests to ensure our thriving House system remains competitive.

Over **(new paragraph)** 80 sports competitions take place over the school year, and include the following activities: **(insert colon)** netball, hockey, **(insert comma)** football, basketball, volleyball and dodgeball. Students are also able to earn points for their House via whole school events such as the Fundraiser Walk, **(insert comma)** through attendance competitions, and by collecting merits, which is an integral part of our rewards system at Grange Hill School. **(insert full stop)**

At Easter, we award the Lombardo **(capital letter)** Trophy to the House earning the most points from sports competitions over the year. At the end of the summer term the Merit Shield is awarded to the House with the most points from students gaining the highest number of Merit Certificates (from the Bronze Certificate to the Headteacher's **(insert apostrophe)** Award) **(close brackets)**.

At the beginning of each year, the students in each House vote for a male and female Sports Captain for each year group. In addition, each form will vote for a Form Representative.   The Form Representative's **(insert**

apostrophe either before or after the letter s) main role is to attend student council meetings throughout the year, and report back to their form on discussions and decisions reached by the School Council.

<u>Grammar</u>

Task 1 – DCA

Task 2 – ADB

Task 3 – CABD

<u>Reading Comprehension</u>

Task 1 – B and E

Task 2 – BDFG

Task 3 – 1C, 2A, 3E, 4G

Task 4 – most relevant – E, least relevant – H

Literacy test 3

<u>Spelling</u>

1. occurrence
2. independent
3. committee
4. perseverance
5. library
6. indispensable
7. maintenance
8. accommodate
9. misspell
10. separate

<u>Punctuation</u>

Exam timetable

This year, **(insert comma)** the GCSE exam period runs from May 13 to June 18. Please remember that you need to remain available to sit exams until June 26, as the exam boards have nominated this as a 'contingency day' **(close inverted commas)** in the event of a national disruption to exams; your parents / carers were informed of this in the autumn term. You have been given a copy of your exam timetable, but if you need another copy, **(insert comma)** please see Ms **(capital letter)** Smith or call in at the main office.

You should arrive in school before 8.50 for exams timetabled for 9.00 **(insert comma)** and before 1.00pm for exams timetabled for 1.30. Unfortunately, Exam Boards may not accept your paper if you arrive late. **(insert full stop)** If **(capital letter)** you think you are going to be late for an exam, you (or your parent / carer) **(close brackets)** must call school immediately so we can tell you what you need to do in your particular situation.

Exam regulations

The school has to implement a very precise set of rules in all public exams, and we are inspected during each GCSE exam period to ensure we are meeting the standards expected. **(insert full stop)** A **(capital letter)** copy of these regulations for both written and on-screen **(insert hyphen)** tests is attached. The latter is only relevant to students taking GCSE computer science. Please read this information carefully, to ensure you do not inadvertently break the rules and risk disqualification. Please note that no potential technological or web-enabled **(insert hyphen)** source of information **(including (open brackets)** mobile phones, ipods, smart watches), may be taken into the exam room. Possession of such a device could result in disqualification, **(insert comma)** even if it's **(insert apostrophe)** switched off and you do not intend to use it.

Grammar

Task 1 – BCDD

Task 2 – ACD

Task 3 – BCB

Reading Comprehension

Task 1 – DG

Task 2 – BEGH

Task 3 – A – NE, B – S, C – EC, D – I

Task 4 – 1C, 2D

Literacy test 4

<u>Spelling</u>

1. occasionally
2. personnel
3. receipts
4. changeable
5. referred
6. references
7. mischievous
8. pronunciation
9. relevant
10. rhythm

<u>Punctuation</u>

Performance Sports Programme

Specialist high-level **(insert hyphen)** coaching, as part of a Performance Sports Programme, **(insert comma)** is provided for those students wishing to pursue their chosen sport and represent that sport at county level or above.

Sports options in the programme include: **(insert colon)** athletics, basketball, cricket, football, rugby, netball, **(insert comma)** hockey and swimming. **(insert full stop)**

Each student's **(insert apostrophe)** programme follows a unique scheme of work, including the latest tactical, technical, physical and mental training. **(insert full stop)** They **(capital letter)** are designed with a focus on individual talent development, and present opportunities for students to develop their skills right through to UK **(capital letter)** and international competition.

(New paragraph) The Sports Science Centre provides students with a movement-analysis testing and monitoring facility, together with equipment designed for assessing a broad range of health and fitness indicators. The Sports Treatment Centre has world class equipment ranging from underwater treadmills to cryotherapy cold spa baths, to help students' **(add apostrophe)** rehabilitation and post-training **(insert hyphen)** recovery.

Importantly, **(insert comma)** all Performance Sport students are enrolled within the Faculty, where the flexibility of the curriculum allows them to combine their sporting programme with a range of options in GCSE, **(insert comma)** A-level and BTEC courses in both Key Stages 4 and 5. This enables them to maintain a well-rounded **(insert hyphen)** education whilst pursuing their passion. They also have access to a strong network of pastoral and academic support, including Tutors, Heads of Year, and Academic Learning Mentors.

Grammar

Task 1 – CAAB

Task 2 – CDC

Task 3 – CCA

Reading Comprehension

Task 1 – BDGH

Task 2 – A and D

Task 3 – 4E, 5D, 10A, 11G

Task 4 – A and D

Printed in Great
Britain
by Amazon

31538776R00077